ORIT SEN-GUPTA

VIJÑĀNA YOGA
PRACTICE MANUAL

VIJNANA BOOKS
www.vijnanayoga.org

Seventh Edition, printed September 2012

VIJNANA BOOKS
WWW.VIJNANAYOGA.ORG
ORIT.SEN@GMAIL.COM

Vijnana Yoga
Practicing, feeling, understanding - from inside

Sources for the term Vijnana:

Vijñāna, विज्ञान - *the act of distinguishing or discerning, understanding, recognizing; intelligence, knowledge, skill, art, science*

(Monier Williams Sanskrit-English Dictionary)

"Verily, different from and within the sheath consisting of mind (manas) is the atma consisting of vijnana (understanding). This has the form of a person...

Faith (śraddhā) is its head,
Order (ṛta) is its right side.
Truth (satya) is its left side.
Yoga is its body.
The Great Intelligence (mahat) is its lower part, the foundation."

(Taittirīya Upaniṣad II.4.1)

"At the stage of mind (manas), we accept authority which is external. At the stage of vijnana, internal growth is affected. We develop faith, order, truthfulness and union with the supreme."

(from S. Radhakrishnan's commentary on the Taittirīya Upaniṣad)

'Yoga is to be known by yoga, yoga leads to yoga,
He who is tireless in yoga delights in yoga for long.'

Patañjali Yoga Sūtras, III.6, Vyāsa's Commentary

For years now, many of us have attempted to deal creatively with the question: "What kind of yoga do you do?"

The 'Full Program' outlined in the second part of this practice manual was taught to me by Dona Holleman and presented in the book "Dancing the Body of Light". Dona told me that this was the teaching she received from Mr. B.K.S. Iyengar when she studied and practiced with him in the sixties.

For me, yoga is yoga, period. This is why we have never had a name other than yoga. It is so important to keep things simple, to be unencumbered by title, hierarchy or organization, so that the tradition which we have been taught can continue to pass on alive, free and in its true form.
And yet, as many of us struggled with increasingly frequent requests by students and friends to define and name our 'type' of yoga, we realized that simply calling it yoga had become insufficient, and even confusing.
In the search for a viable solution, names came up, there were discussions, but nothing seemed to be 'it' and to decide arbitrarily on this or that name felt artificial.

Then the term Vijnana (understanding, discerning) came up. We had studied the Taittiriya Upanishad where the human being and the Cosmos are described as having five koshas, or layers: the physical, the energetic, the mental, the 'vijnanic' and the joyous.

Sri Aurobindo, in The Synthesis of Yoga, expounds at length on the Vijnana Kosha and writes, among other things, that as directly as physical vision sees and grasps the appearance of objects, even more so does vijnana see and grasp the truth of things.

This state of seeing and understanding seems to resonate with a way of being, seeing and acting that is both the means and the objective of our yoga practice.

Through our practice of sitting, pranayama, asana and the study of texts, we aspire to refine and integrate the body, mind, heart and consciousness. The guiding principles of relaxing the body, quieting the mind, focusing through intent, rooting, connecting, expanding and an awareness of breathing allow us to go deep within and from that place to see, to feel, to understand and to act skillfully.

Calling our way of practicing Vijnana Yoga is but giving recognition to something that has always been there, something that is at the core of our discipline: practicing, feeling, understanding - from inside.

Many thanks to all my teachers for persistently pointing their fingers at this one moon.

Orit Sen-Gupta, December 2003, Jerusalem.

Note: Three years of practicing together have elapsed, and we are republishing the Practice Manual in an enriched version. Galya Shalit has kindly created drawings of the asanas. I hope that her long labor of love, which began as a project in the Teacher Training Course, will make the manual more user-friendly.

VIJNANA YOGA PRACTICE MANUAL

CONTENTS   PAGE

A. Introduction

B. Daily Practice

C. Intermediate Program

Morning Practice

Afternoon Practice

Health Precautions

This manual is in no way meant to serve as a means for learning Prāṇāyāma or Āsāna. It is intended that it be used in conjunction with live study, preferably with a teacher who has learned and practices by this system.

In case you are suffering from any medical problems or chronic illness, have recently had surgery, given birth or are pregnant, it is imperative that you consult with both a yoga teacher and a physician before practicing Prāṇāyāma or Āsāna according to this Practice Manual.

A Note on Pronunciation

The following is a partial guide to the pronunciation of Sanskrit transliteration.

Vowels:

a	like the u in hut	example: Eka Pāda
ā	like the a in father	example: Prāṇāyāma, Āsāna
i	like the i in sit	example: Piṇḍāsana
ī	like the ee in sleep	example: Pīncha Mayūrāsana, Viparīta
u	like the u in put	example: Adho Mukha
ū	like the oo in hoot	example: Mūla Bandha
ṛ	like the ri in rich	example: Vṛkṣāsana, Parivṛtta
ai	like the i in smile	example: Bhairavāsana
o	like the o in home	example: Baddha Koṇāsana

Consonaṇts:

ś and ṣ	like the sh in ship	example: Pārśva, Uṣṭrāsana, Śīrṣāsana
th	like the th in pothole	example: Jaṭhara, Haṭha Yoga
c and ch	like the ch in chair	example: Chaturanga, Citta

In general, syllables with long vowels (ā, ī, ū) are accented, receiving stress, as in Samādhi, Viparīta, Ūrdhva Dhanurāsana.

Guidelines for Practice

Fifteen years ago I spent some time in a small mountain monastery in the Galilee. One of the Christian monks there did yoga and asked me what my daily practice was. I was embarrassed, as I had no clear answer. After 11 years of being a committed yoga student I hadn't yet been initiated into the secrets of a steady daily practice.

Intuitively I realized the great lack. The so-called freedom to choose each day what to do, the absence of clear guidelines that give direction and a framework, was more a burden than a joy.

Afterwards, when I met Dona Holleman and began to practice with her, I felt gratitude for the simplicity and the clarity of a defined daily practice. There was wholeness to each of the practices, and a weekly framework that held them together in a proper balance. It was for me the perfect outlet and means to express the yearning of the heart.

Dona explained to me that this was how she had learned yoga from Mr. Iyengar when she first began to study with him in the sixties. Every day in the morning there was Prāṇāyāma then Āsana (each day a different group of Āsanas) and in the afternoon Headstand and Shoulder Stand. Till today I practice as I learned from my teacher, body to body, and still find the practice stimulating and refining, a teaching in itself.

The heart of yoga is practice. When yoga is practiced correctly and continuously over an extended period of time with devotion, its secrets reveal themselves, supporting and enriching us. From the firmness of posture, to the steadiness of mind, to a refined breath, yoga uplifts us day by day in our most minute ways of being and functioning.

Over the years the way of practice as elaborated in this Practice Manual has become the practice of many. For those who have undertaken this way as well as for their students the Practice Manual has been reorganized and slightly modified. The main objective has been to clarify the daily practice itself.

When we place the Practice Manual beside the mat, we need to regard its instructions as guidelines and not rules. Many of us have benefited from the systemizing of the practice. Even so this is an 'Open Manual'. Though there are directives concerning the order of the Āsanas and the days on which they are to be practiced, we need to be watchful that the outcome of this order will not be fundamentalism or rigidity.

For yoga to blossom, listening and responding to what one hears from inside is the golden rule. Within the framework created, there is space for adapting the practice to the particular needs of the day or the person. There is always place to change the order of some of the sequences or the days on which they are practiced, to practice softly or more vigorously. The poses can be done separately or in Vinyasa or with Sūrya Namaskar or in a combination of the last two. This, according to the different needs of each person, day by day.

It is important to remember that the mere repetition of the various daily practices is not enough. The quality of the practice depends on a deep listening and responding to the body, heart and mind.

The Principles are that deep listening and constant response through subtle adjustments. They are the very core of practice. Relaxing, intensifying the mind, focusing through intent, rooting, connecting and an awareness of the breath are not ideas or tools; they are a way of being, of functioning.

Using the Practice Manual without applying the principles may lead to a technical and shallow practice at best. There can also be the more unpleasant outcome of injuries if we treat yogic practices as mere physical techniques.

Finally, yoga practice is not isolated from our everyday life. What we ate yesterday, when we went to sleep, our relationships at work and home, all these walk with us onto the mat and ask for attention and readjustment. The very fabric of our personal lives is the material for our practice. It is this fabric that meets the fire of practice and the intensity of heart.

Thus the mat becomes a place of meeting between the deep waters of our spirit - the eternal spark within us - and our persona, our life. On the way to the depths or on the way back, we are in middle waters; in these, skillfulness and presence of mind are of utmost importance. By enhancing the fire of practice to bring light to these areas of the self, by not shunning or avoiding these spaces, our practice becomes a daily attempt to connect the deep within to the whole of ourselves.

This has always been the goal of yoga: to connect the upper and lower worlds and rediscover the inherent oneness of all life.

"All Life is Yoga", says Śri Aurobindo.

May the use of this manual be a small step towards the understanding of that.

Jerusalem 2001

The Principles

1. Relaxing the Body

In the beginning, relax the body. Inhale, and with the exhalation release tension. Inhale, and with the following exhalation scan the body from top to bottom and from the bottom upwards.

Wherever there is gripping or tension - relax.

The mind is looking at the body with a parental eye. With time one can observe tense areas releasing and embracing space. If areas of weakness are noticed, inhale into them with courage and enliven them with energy. Let excess leave the body; relax. Thus the body becomes stable and quiet.

2. Quieting the Mind

When we position ourselves on the mat we distance ourselves from our responsibility to react to the world. The eyes look inward to catch the inner mood, the state of mind.

Whether we are concentrated, dispersed or nervous; happy, sad or angry; whether we are afraid, tired or energetic - the eyes are positioned at the back of the head.

We observe ourselves and our practice from an inner silence. With each inhalation the eyes sink deeper into the back of the head. With each exhalation there is an intensification of concentration.

Empty Mind intensifies itself in practice.

3. Intent

Now the body and mind are at ease and stable, quiet and concentrated. From this place we see our objective - Sitting, Prāṇāyāma, Āsana - and direct ourselves towards it.

The mind directs itself to the practice; the body awaits the practice; the heart embraces the practice with all its might.

With each inhalation there is an intensification of intent, with each exhalation the sharpening of its direction. By visualizing ourselves sitting, breathing, moving, or by imagining another person in that practice we devote ourselves wholly to it. With each breath, with each pose we reaffirm our intent.

4. Rooting

The mind rests at the place where the body touches the earth. Let the weight of the body sink into this place - for example, the feet. Intensify the weight pressing down, as if the foot would like to sink into the earth, and then feel the power of that downward movement flowing through the body. As the roots of a tree deepen and widen into the earth, so the branches above expand into the sky.

It is easy to understand the idea behind rooting, yet surprisingly difficult to execute it in every movement and posture. As rooting is mastered, the body becomes light and loose and moves without effort.

5. Connecting

Always be conscious of two opposite directions that are connected to each other. To go up, go down. To go forwards, shift into the back. Wishing for the left side, steady yourself on the right. Wishing to expand, come from the core.

The first direction is the arrow, the second direction is the bow; the thread which binds them is Connecting. In each pose the farthest limb from the ground connects to that which is rooting into the ground.

Every single body part in between is whole in itself, a distinct, functioning unit. All the parts are balanced and work together in harmony.

Like a chain floating in space, the rings that make up the chain never touch each other. The more each part is distinct, the more the connection between them remains steady - the body in any situation moves in oneness.

6. Breathing

Be aware of inhaling, of exhaling. Inhale - go deep within; exhale - connect to the world. Inhale - accept what is; exhale - give yourself to the earth.
Inhale along the body, exhale and root. Inhale and connect the farthest parts, exhale and move into the final pose.

While inhaling the body elongates and widens, while exhaling it steadies itself in rooting and connecting. At times the breath is sweet and soft, at times it is deep and long. Sometimes the exhalation lasts longer than the inhalation, sometimes it is short and decisive.

At times only in the background, at times the source of action, breath is always present.

7. Expanding - Elongating and Widening

When there is rooting while exhaling, inhaling brings about elongation and widening. Or perhaps the elongating and widening, that occur as a result of rooting, allow for inhalation.

When elongating and widening occur, not one ring touches another as the chain called body moves in space. Then there is no sagging into the joints, no effort in the muscles. The skeleton shields its coverings, the coverings create space for the skeleton. Thus the body moves about - relaxed and connected - one.

Finally

All the principles coexist and need to be applied at all times, yet it is difficult to oversee their functions simultaneously. In order to deepen our understanding of the principles, we need to choose one that attracts us and work with it constantly until it is mastered. Many times we can work with one or two principles for a few years until these penetrate and become second nature to us.

This while remembering that it is only when all the principles coexist simultaneously in practice, that the practice is whole. Therefore when we practice yet feel 'stuck' we need to look carefully and find which principle is neglected, and then revive it.

Just Sitting - Dhyāna

The instruction is, to sit every day, in a good posture, for a regular length of time:

Sit in a comfortable position, the back effortlessly erect, the sitting bones seated on the ground, on a cushion or on a folded blanket.

If we look at the body from the side, the shoulder is above the pelvis, the ear above the shoulder, the back at ease. The spinal column is not tilted either to the left or to the right, neither forward nor backwards.

The eyes are closed gently, and can be opened at times. The gaze is turned inwards. The back of the neck is long and wide.

While sitting, we create a neutral space, in which consciousness can return to its own form.[1]

At first we may see endless feelings, emotions and thoughts; we may have to deal with fatigue, agitation, boredom and frustration. Unpleasant and pleasant memories may occur; we may discover within ourselves fears of the future.

The very watching, patiently, of whatever comes up within us - that is the practice. With time, consciousness becomes clearer, sharper, and deepens into itself. Concentration intensifies into meditation, until "that shines forth as the object only".[2]

---

[1] tadā draṣṭuḥ sva-rūpe'vasthānam - "Then the dwelling of the See'er in his own form." The Yoga Sūtras of Patañjali, chapter I, sūtra 3

[2] tad-eva-artha-mātra-nirbhāsaṃ sva-rūpa-śūnya-iva-samādiḥ - "When that shines forth as the object only, as if (consciousness is) empty of its own form - Samādhi." The Yoga Sūtras of Patañjali, chapter III, sūtra 3

Kriyās and Prāṇāyāma

Kriyās and Prāṇāyāma should always be practiced carefully and gently, never overstraining the lungs or nervous system. Limit yourself to no more than 45 minutes a day of these practices.

The Kriyās can be done all together in the early morning before or after evacuation.

Prāṇāyāma is usually done in the morning before the Āsanas. A short break should be taken between Prāṇāyāma and Āsana practice.

Each of the Prāṇāyāma exercises should be practiced for no more then 10 minutes at a time. Choose three Prāṇāyāma exercises each morning. Refine gradually the practice of the bandhas in Prāṇāyāma - Mūla Bandha, Uḍḍīyāna Bandha and Jālandhara Bandha.

Remember that overly strenuous practice of Prāṇāyāma may lead to irritability and over sensitivity in general. Pregnant women and people with chronic medical problems should avoid the Kriyās and breath-retention.

Kriyās

- **Uḍḍīyāna Bandha** - 3 cycles
- **Agni Sara** - 3 cycles (3-25 times each)
- **Nauli** - 3 cycles (3-50 times each)

Prāṇāyāma

1. Kapālabhāti

a. Gentle Kapālabhāti I - 1 min. cycle (Inhale 5 sec.→ Kapālabhāti 15 sec.→ inhale 10 sec.→ kumbhaka 20 sec.→ exhale 10 sec.) Repeat up to 10 times.

b. Gentle Kapālabhāti II (gradual lengthening and shortening of kumbhaka)

c. Classical Kapālabhāti (1 minute x 3 of Kapālabhāti)

d. Continuous Kapālabhāti (3-5 minutes and then Kumbhaka)

e. Nāḍī Śodhana Kapālabhāti I (the nostrils are kept open in Kapālabhāti)

f. Nāḍī Śodhana Kapālabhāti II (one nostril is closed during Kapālabhāti)

2. Ujjāyi

a. Inhalation and Exhalation
b. Inhalation, Antara Kumbhaka, Exhalation
c. Sama-vṛtti of a. and b.
d. Exhalation double of Inhalation, gradually lengthening Antara Kumbaka
e. Sama-vṛtti of Inhalation, Antara Kumbhaka, Exhalation, Bāhya Kumbhaka

3. Anuloma Viloma

a. Gradual Inhalation, Smooth Exhalation
b. Smooth Inhalation, Gradual Exhalation
c. Gradual Inhalation, Gradual Exhalation

4. Nāḍī Śodhana

a. Gentle Nāḍī Śodhana I (without hands)
b. Gentle Nāḍī Śodhana II (hands on the back and chest)
c. Nāḍī Śodhana with two hands - Sama-vṛtti
d. Classical Nāḍī Śodhana with one hand
(rhythms: 1:1, 1:2, 1:1:2, 1:2:2, 1:4:2:1)

5. Sūrya Bhedana

Inhale through the right, Kumbhaka, Exhale through the left.

❖ Note: There are other Prāṇāyāma practices which are not mentioned here.

INTERMEDIATE PROGRAM

"Yoga-Siddhi, the perfection that comes from the practice of Yoga, can be best attained by the combined workings of four great instruments.

There is, first, the knowledge of the truths, principles, powers and processes that govern the realization - ***Shastra.***

Next comes a patient and persistent action on the lines laid down by the knowledge, the force of our personal effort - ***Utsaha.***

There intervenes, third, uplifting our knowledge and effort into the domain of spiritual experience, the direct suggestion, example and influence of the Teacher - ***Guru.***

Last comes the instrumentality of Time - ***Kala***; for in all things there is a cycle of their action and a period of the divine movement."

Śri Aurobindo - The Synthesis of Yoga, p. 47

STANDING POSES - Intermediate Program (Sunday)

These poses can be done in three different modes:

A. Performing each pose separately.

B. The Eight Forms:

1. Sūrya Namaskar I : Tāḍāsana → Uttānāsana → Chaturanga Daṇḍāsana → Ūrdhva Mukha Śvānāsana → Adho Mukha Śvānāsana → Uttānāsana → Tāḍāsana.
2. Sūrya Namaskar II : Tāḍāsana → Utkaṭāsana → Uttānāsana → Chaturanga Daṇḍāsana → Ūrdhva Mukha Śvānāsana → Adho Mukha Śvānāsana → Vīrabhadrāsana I → Chaturanga Daṇḍāsana → Ūrdhva Mukha Śvānāsana → Adho Mukha Śvānāsana → Uttānāsana → Utkaṭāsana → Tāḍāsana.
3. Uttānāsana cycle : three variations (feet apart and holding the big toe, feet apart and palms under feet, feet together and holding the ankles).
4. Vṛkṣāsana cycle : Vṛkṣāsana I → Vṛkṣāsana II → Garuḍāsana.
5. Trikoṇāsana cycle : Utthita Trikoṇāsana → Ardha Chandrāsana → Parivṛtta Ardha Chandrāsana → Parivṛtta Trikoṇāsana → Pārśvottānāsana → Eka Pāda Uttānāsana → Uttānāsana →Tāḍāsana.
6. Vīrabhadrāsana I cycle : Vīrabhadrāsana I → Vīrabhadrāsana III → Utthita Hasta Pādānguṣṭhāsana (first the leg forwards and then to the side).
7. Vīrabhadrāsana II cycle :Vīrabhadrāsana II → Utthita Pārśvakoṇāsana → Parivṛtta Pārśvakoṇāsana.
8. Prasārita Pādottānāsana cycle : three variations.

C. Vinyasa I - Connecting two or more poses by flowing from one into the other.

D. Vinyasa II - Interlacing all the poses with Sūrya Namaskar.

The Poses:

1. **Tāḍāsana**
   tāḍa=mountain
2. **Utkaṭāsana**
   utkata=powerful, fierce
3. **Garuḍāsana** - 1 minute
   garuḍa=eagle

1 Sūrya Namaskar I

2 Sūrya Namaskar II

3 Uttānāsana cycle

4 Vṛkṣāsana cycle

5 Trikoṇāsana cycle

6 Vīrabhadrāsana I cycle

7 Vīrabhadrāsana II cycle

8 Prasārita Pādottānāsana cycle

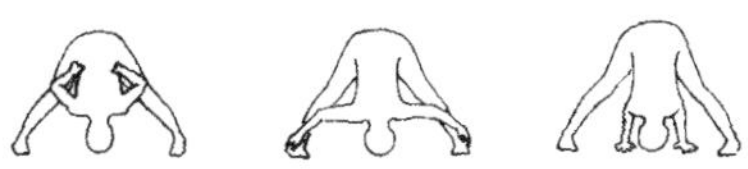

****

Tāḍāsana

Utkaṭāsana

Garuḍāsana

4. **Vṛkṣāsana I** - 1 minute
vṛkṣa=tree
5. **Vṛkṣāsana II** - 1 minute

6. **Utthita Trikoṇāsana** - 1 minute
utthita=extended; tri=three; koṇa=angle; trikoṇa=triangle
7. **Ardha Chandrāsana** - 1 minute
ardha=half; chandra=moon
8. **Pārśvottānāsana** - 1 minute
pārśva=side, flank; uttana=intense stretch
9. **Parivṛtta Trikoṇāsana** - 1 minute
parivṛtta=turned around; trikoṇa=triangle
10. **Parivṛtta Ardha Chandrāsana** - 1 minute

11. **Vīrabhadrāsana II** - 1 minute
Vīrabhadra is the name of a hero
12. **Utthita Pārśvakoṇāsana** - 1 minute
utthita=extended; pārśva=sideways; koṇa=angle
13. **Parivṛtta Pārśvakoṇāsana** - 1 minute
parivṛtta=turned around; pārśva=sideways; koṇa=angle
14. **Vīrabhadrāsana I** - 1 minute

15. **Vīrabhadrāsana III**

16. **Utthita Hasta Pādānguṣṭhāsana**
utthita=extended; hasta=hand; pādāṅguṣṭha=big toe
a. Holding the foot with the same side hand - 1 minute
b. Holding the foot with the same side hand and bringing it to the side - 30 seconds
c. Leg in the air
17. **Eka Pāda Uttānāsana** - 30 seconds
eka=one; pāda=leg, foot; uttana=intense stretch
18. **Prasārita Pādottānāsana** (three variations)
prasārita=spread, extended; pāda=leg, foot; uttana=intense stretch
19. **Uttānāsana**
uttana=intense stretch
a. Catching big toe - 1 minute
b. Palms under feet - 1 minute
c. Holding ankles - 1 minute

~ Śavāsana ~

Vṛkṣāsana I

Vṛkṣāsana II

Utthita Trikoṇāsana

Ardha Chandrāsana

Pārśvottānāsana

Parivṛtta
Trikoṇāsana

Parivrtta
Ardha Chandrasana

Vīrabhadrāsana II

Utthita
Pārśvakoṇāsana

Parivrtta
Pārśvakoṇāsana

Vīrabhadrāsana I

Vīrabhadrāsana III

a b c
Utthita Hasta Pādānguṣṭhāsana

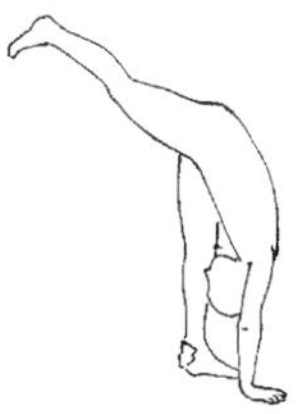

Eka Pāda Uttānāsana

a b c
Prasārita Pādottānāsana

a b c
Uttānāsana

HAND BALANCES - Intermediate Program (Monday)

These poses can be done in three different modes:

A. **Performing each pose separately.**
B. **Vinyasa I** - Connecting two or more poses by flowing from one into the other.
C. **Vinyasa II** - Interlacing all the poses with Sūrya Namaskar.

The Poses: (Explanations for the āsana names are given on p. 29.)

1. **Adho Mukha Śvānāsana** - 1 minute
2. **Adho Mukha Vṛkṣāsana** - 1 minute
3. **Pīncha Mayūrāsana** - 1 minute
4. **Vasiṣṭhāsana I** - 30 seconds
5. **Vasiṣṭhāsana II** - 30 seconds
6. **Kaśyapāsana** - 30 seconds
7. **Viśvāmitrāsana** - 30 seconds
8. **Dwi Hasta Bhujāsana**
9. **Tittibhāsana**
10. **Bhujapidāsana**
11. **Eka Hasta Bhujāsana, Aṣṭāvakrāsana**
12. **Bakāsana** (from floor or from Headstand II)
13. **Pārśva Bakāsana** (from floor or from Headstand II)
14. **Eka Pāda Bakāsana II** (from floor or Headstand II)
15. **Setu Bandha** x3
16. **Paschimottānāsana** 5-10 minutes

~ **Śavāsana** ~

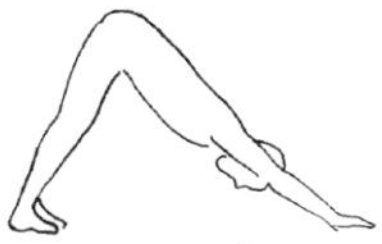
Adho Mukha Śvānāsana

Adho Mukha Vṛkṣāsana

Pīncha Mayūrāsana

Vasiṣṭhāsana I

Vasiṣṭhāsana II

Kaśyapāsana

Viśvāmitrāsana

Dwi Hasta Bhujāsana

Tittibhāsana

Bhujapidāsana

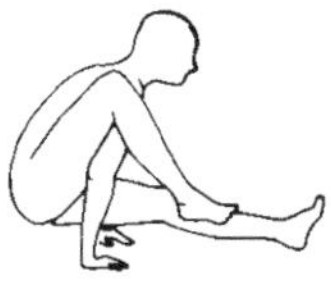
Eka Hasta Bhujāsana

Aṣṭāvakrāsana

Bakāsana

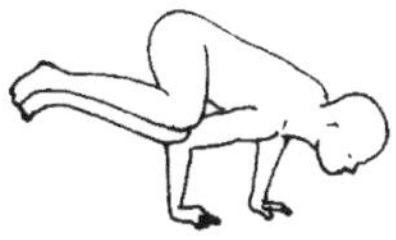
Pārśva Bakāsana

Eka Pāda Bakāsana II

Setu Bandha

Paschimottānāsana

SIMPLE BACKBENDS - Intermediate Program (Tuesday)

These poses can be done in three different modes:

A. **Performing each pose separately.**
B. **Vinyasa I** - Connecting two or more poses by flowing from one into the other.
C. **Vinyasa II** - Interlacing all the poses with Sūrya Namaskar.

The Poses:

1. **Adho Mukha Śvānāsana** - 1 minute
2. **Adho Mukha Vṛkṣāsana** - 1 minute
3. **Pīncha Mayūrāsana** - 1 minute

4. **Eka Pāda Śalabhāsana**
   eka=one; pāda=leg, foot
   a. Arms forwards, same side arm and leg up x3
   b. Arms forwards, opposite arm and leg up x3

5. **Ūrdhva Mukha Śalabhāsana**
   ūrdhva=upwards; mukha=face; salabha=locust
   a. Arms backwards x3
   b. Arms sideways x3
   c. Arms forwards x3
   d. Makarāsana x3
   makara=crocodile

6. **Dwi Pāda Śalabhāsana**
   dwi=two; pāda=leg, foot
   a. Head and arms on the ground x3
   b. Arms backwards x3
   c. Arms sideways x3
   d. Arms forwards x3
   e. Makarāsana x3
   makara=crocodile

7. **Dhanurāsana** x3
   dhanu=bow

8. **Bhujaṅgāsana**
   bhujaṅga=serpent

9. **Ūrdhva Mukha Śvānāsana**
   ūrdhva=upwards; mukha=face; ṣvāna=dog

Adho Mukha Śvānāsana

Adho Mukha Vṛkṣāsana

Pincha Mayurasana

Eka Pāda Śalabhāsana

Ūrdhva Mukha Śalabhāsana

Dwi Pāda Śalabhāsana

Dhanurāsana

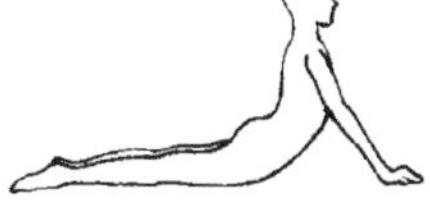

Bhujaṇgāsana

Ūrdhva Mukha Śvānāsana

10. **Uṣṭrāsana**
uṣṭra=camel

11. **Setu Bandha** - 1-5 minutes

12. **Eka Pāda Setu Bandha**
eka=one; pāda=leg, foot

Leg Stretches - Short Timing (Tuesday, Thursday)

1. **Ūrdhva Mukha Paschimottānāsana II** - 1 minute
(legs together, holding feet with hands)
ūrdhva=upwards; mukha=face; paschima=the west, the back of the body; uttana=intense stretch

2. **Ūrdhva Mukha Prasārita Pādottānāsana II** - 1 minute
(legs spread, holding feet with hands)
prasārita=extended; pāda=leg, foot; uttana=intense stretch

3. **Supta Pādānguṣṭhāsana I** - 1 minute
(holding right leg with both hands)
supta=lying down; pādāṅguṣṭha=big toe

4. **Supta Pādānguṣṭhāsana II** - 1 minute
(with right hand bring right foot to right side)

5. **Supta Pādānguṣṭhāsana III** - 1 minute
(with left hand bring right foot to left side)

6. **Anantāsana** - 1 minute
ananta=infinite

7. **Repeat 3 through 6 with the left leg.**

~ Śavāsana ~

Uṣṭrāsana

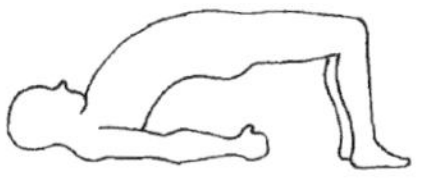

Setu Bandha

Eka Pāda Setu Bandha

LEG STRECHES

Urdhva Mukha
Paschimottānāsana II

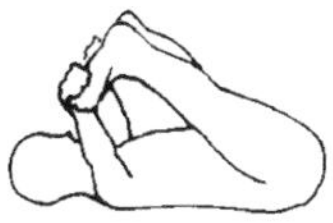

Urdhva Mukha
Prasārita Padottānāsana II

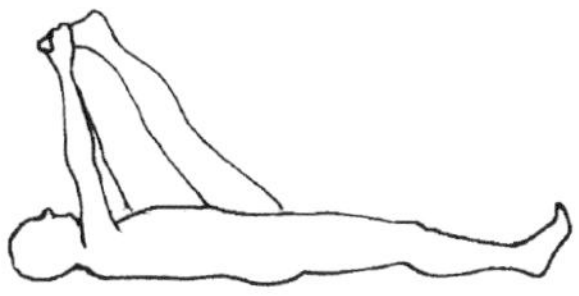

Supta Pādānguṣṭhāsana I

Supta Pādānguṣṭhāsana II

Supta Pādānguṣṭhāsana III

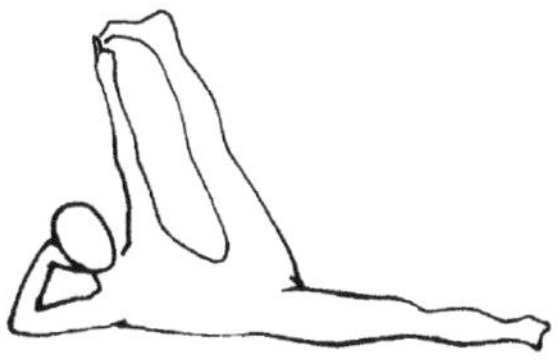

Anantāsana

FORWARD BENDS - Intermediate Program (Wednesday)

These poses can be done in four different modes:

A. Performing each pose separately.
B. Vinyasa I - Connecting two or more poses, flowing from one to the other.
C. Vinyasa II - Interlacing all the poses with Sūrya Namaskar.
D. Vinyasa III - A variation of Vinyasa I & II in which the twists are included.

Vinyasa III: (Explanations for the āsana names are given on p. 33.)

1. **Sūrya Namaskar I** - x3
2. **Uttānāsana** - (3 variations)
3. **Paschimottānāsana**
   - Daṇḍāsana - 1 minute
   - 3 variations: elongating upwards 1 min, coming forwards 1 min
   - Pūrvottānāsana - 30 seconds
4. **Jānu Śīrṣāsana**
   - **a.** twisting and elongating upwards - 1 minute
   - **b.** coming forwards - 1 minute
   - **c.** Parivṛtta Jānu Śīrṣāsana - 1 minute
5. **Ardha Baddha Padma Paschimottānāsana**
   - **a.** twisting and elongating upwards - 1 minute
   - **b.** coming forwards - 1 minute
   - **c.** Parivṛtta Eka Pāda Padmāsana - 1 minute
6. **Triang Mukhaikapāda Paschimottānāsana**
   - **a.** twisting and elongating upwards - 1 minute
   - **b.** coming forwards - 1 minute
   - **c.** Marīchyāsana IV - 1 minute
7. **Krounchāsana**
   - **a.** head away from shin - 1 minute
   - **b.** head to shin - 1 minute
   - **c.** Bharadvājāsana II - 1 minute
8. **Marīchyāsana I**
   - **a.** twisting and elongating upwards - 1 minute
   - **b.** coming forwards - 1 minute
   - **c.** Marīchyāsana III - 1 minute
9. **Upaviṣṭha Koṇāsana**
   - **a.** elongating upwards - 1 minute
   - **b.** coming forwards - 1 minute
10. **Baddha Koṇāsana**
    - **a.** elongating upwards - 1 minute
    - **b.** coming forwards - 1 minute
11. **Parivṛtta Ardha Padmāsana** or **Parivṛtta Padmāsana** - 1 minute
12. **Bharadvājāsana I** - 1 minute
13. **Pāśāsana** - 1 minute
14. **Ardha Matsyendrāsana** - 1 minute

~ **Śavāsana** ~

Uttānāsana

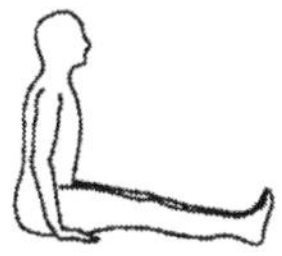

Daṇḍāsana

Paschimottānāsana

Pūrvottānāsana

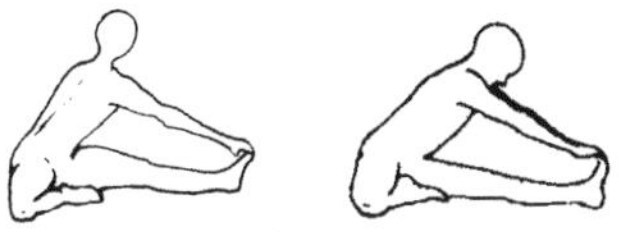

Jānu Śīrṣāsana

Parivṛtta
Jānu Śīrṣāsana

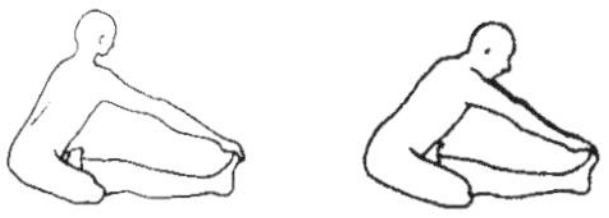

Ardha Baddha Padma
Paschimottānāsana

Parivṛtta Eka Pāda
Padmāsana

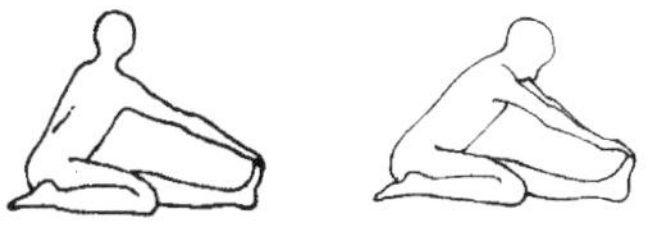

Triang Mukhaikapāda
Paschimottānāsana

Marīchyāsana IV

Krounchāsana

Bharadvājāsana II

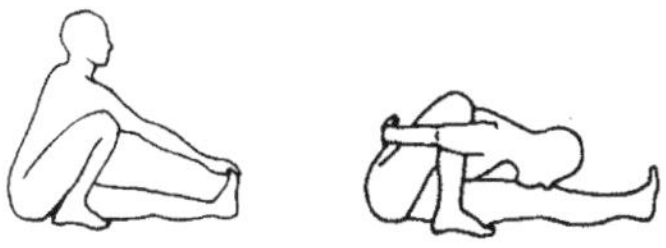

Marīchyāsanaa I

Marīchyāsana III

Upaviṣṭha Koṇāsana

Baddha Koṇāsana

Parivṛtta Padmāsana

Bharadvājāsana I

Pāśāsana

Ardha Matsyendrāsana

BACKBEND VARIATIONS - Intermediate Program (Thursday)

These poses can be done in two different modes:

A. Performing each pose separately.

B. Vinyasa - Interlacing all the poses with Sūrya Namaskar.

The Poses: (Explanations for the āsana names are given on p. 38.)

1. **Adho Mukha Śvānāsana** - 1 minute
2. **Adho Mukha Vṛkṣāsana** - 1 minute
3. **Pīncha Mayūrāsana** - 1 minute
4. **Ūrdhva Dhanurāsana** - x6 (pushing up from floor)
5. **Dwi Pāda Viparīta Daṇḍāsana** - x3 (pushing up from floor)
6. **Viparīta Daṇḍāsana** (going back from headstand to wall or to floor)
7. **Eka Pāda Rājakapotāsana I** (the position of the legs only)
8. **Eka Pāda Rājakapotāsana II** (the position of the legs only)
9. **Ūrdhva Dhanurāsana** (going back to wall or to floor)
10. **Uttānāsana** - 1 minute
11. **Squat or Bakāsana**

Leg Stretches - Short Timing (Tuesday, Thursday)

1. **Ūrdhva Mukha Paschimottānāsana II** - 1 minute
(legs together, holding feet with hands).
2. **Ūrdhva Mukha Prasārita Pādottānāsana II** - 1 minute
(legs spread, holding feet with hands).
3. **Supta Pādānguṣṭhāsana I** - 1 minute
(holding right leg with both hands).
4. **Supta Pādānguṣṭhāsana II** - 1 minute
(with right hand bring right foot to right side)
5. **Supta Pādānguṣṭhāsana III** - 1 minute
(with left hand bring right foot to left side)
6. **Anantāsana** - 1 minute

7. **Repeat 3 through 6 with the left leg.**

~ Śavāsana ~

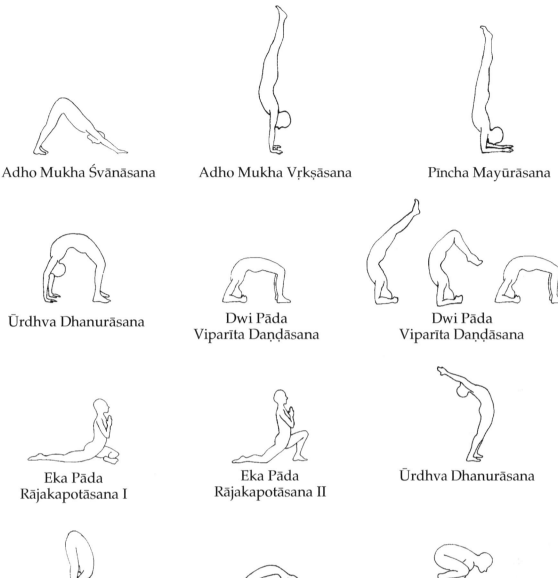

Adho Mukha Śvānāsana

Adho Mukha Vṛkṣāsana

Pīncha Mayūrāsana

Ūrdhva Dhanurāsana

Dwi Pāda
Viparīta Daṇḍāsana

Dwi Pāda
Viparīta Daṇḍāsana

Eka Pāda
Rājakapotāsana I

Eka Pāda
Rājakapotāsana II

Ūrdhva Dhanurāsana

Uttānāsana

Squat

Bakāsana

LEG STRECHES

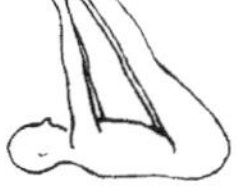

Ūrdhva Mukha
Paschimottānāsana II

Ūrdhva Mukha
Prasārita Padottānāsana II

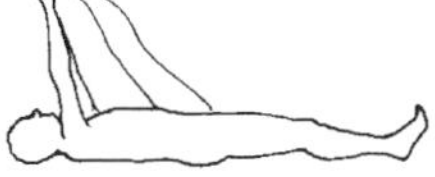

Supta Pādānguṣṭhāsana I

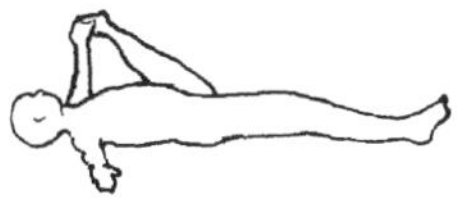

Supta Pādānguṣṭhāsana II

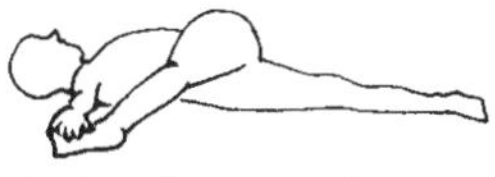

Supta Pādānguṣṭhāsana III

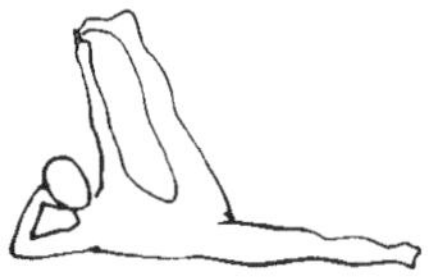

Anantāsana

ON FRIDAY, the following two options of practice are offered:

A. Sūrya Namaskar x 27 up to 108 (Friday)

This practice is concerned with the effects of repetitive flow. In the full program we practice once a week 108 Ūrdhva Dhanurāsana. For intermediate practitioners the effects produced by repetition are created by repeating Sūrya Namaskar many times, slowly increasing up to 108.

B. Vinyasa Practice (Friday)

This option in concerned with the effects of combining together Āsanas from each of the different groups in one practice. The following sequence is an example of such a practice:

1. **Sūrya Namaskar I** - x3
2. **Uttānāsana** - three variations
3. **Adho Mukha Vṛkṣāsana** - 1 minute
4. **Pīncha Mayūrāsana** - 1 minute
5. **Trikoṇāsana cycle:** Utthita Trikoṇāsana → Ardha Chandrāsana → Parivṛtta Ardha Chandrāsana → Parivṛtta Trikoṇāsana → Pārśvottānāsana → Eka Pāda Uttānāsana → Uttānāsana →Tāḍāsana.
6. **Vasiṣṭhāsana I** - 30 seconds
7. **Vasiṣṭhāsana II** - 30 seconds
8. **Tittibhāsana,**
9. **Jānu Śīrṣāsana**
   - **a.** twisting and elongating upwards - 1 minute
   - **b.** coming forwards - 1 minute
   - **c.** Parivṛtta Jānu Śīrṣāsana - 1 minute
10. **Triang Mukhaikapāda Paschimottānāsana**
    - **a.** twisting and elongating upwards - 1 minute
    - **b.** coming forwards - 1 minute
    - **c.** Marīchyāsana IV - 1 minute
11. **Upaviṣṭha Koṇāsana**
12. **Baddha Koṇāsana**
13. **Setu Bandha**
14. **Ūrdhva Dhanurāsana** - x6 (pushing up from floor)
15. **Dwi Pāda Viparīta Daṇḍāsana** - x3 (pushing up from floor)
16. **Leg Stretches**
    - **a.** Ūrdhva Mukha Paschimottānāsana II - 1 minute
    - **b.** Ūrdhva Mukha Prasārita Pādottānāsana II - 1 minute
    - **c.** Supta Pādānguṣṭhāsana I - 1 minute
    - **d.** Supta Pādānguṣṭhāsana II - 1 minute
    - **e.** Supta Pādānguṣṭhāsana III - 1 minute

~ Śavāsana ~

Sūrya Namaskar I

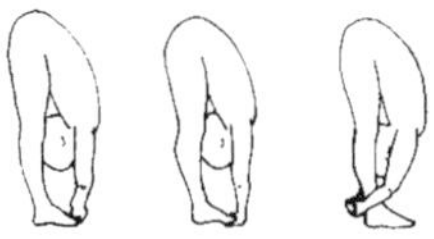

Uttānāsana

Adho Mukha Vṛkṣāsana

Pīncha Mayūrāsana

Trikoṇāsana cycle

Vasiṣṭhāsana I

Vasiṣṭhāsana II

Tittibhāsana

Jānu Śīrṣāsana

Parivṛtta
Jānu Śīrṣāsana

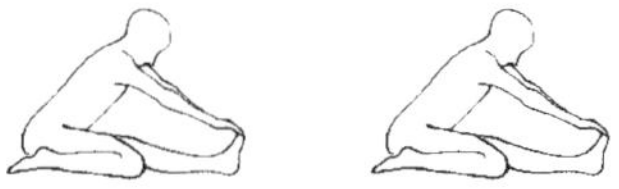

Triang Mukhaikapāda
Paschimottānāsana

Marīchyāsana IV

Upaviṣṭha Koṇāsana

Baddha Koṇāsana

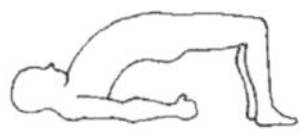

Setu Bandha

Ūrdhva Dhanurāsana

Dwi Pāda
Viparīta Daṇḍāsana

Ūrdhva Mukha
Paschimottānāsana II

Ūrdhva Mukha
Prasārita Padottānāsana II

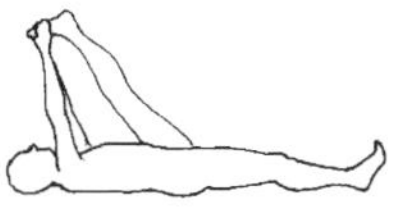

Supta Pādānguṣṭhāsana I

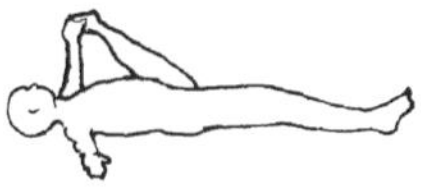

Supta Pādānguṣṭhāsana II

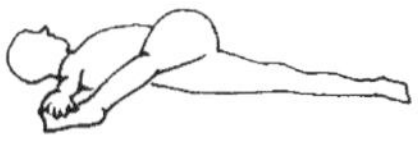

Supta Pādānguṣṭhāsana III

Anantāsana

AFTERNOON PRACTICE - Intermediate Program

The daily afternoon practice includes Nāvāsana poses, the head and shoulder stand cycles and one group of sitting poses. The time spent in the inverted poses, especially headstand, needs to be built up gradually over a long period of time. Once the following practice is stabilized, the rest of the variations from the full program can be added to both Headstand and Shoulder Stand.

Women should avoid headstand and shoulder stand during their menstrual period.

NĀVĀSANA POSES

1. **Ūrdhva Prasārita Pādāsana** - x3
   holding the legs for 30 seconds at 90 degrees, then for 15 seconds at 60 and 30 degrees respectfully
   ūrdhva=upwards; prasārita=extended; pāda=leg, foot

2. **Jaṭhara Parivartanāsana** - 5 times to each side
   jaṭhara=stomach; parivartana=turning, rolling

3. **Nāvāsanas**
   - **A. Ardha Nāvāsana**
     1. **Eka Pāda Ardha Nāvāsana** - x2
     2. **Ardha Nāvāsana** - x2
   - **B. Paripūrṇa Nāvāsana** - x2

   ardha=half; paripūrṇa=full; nāva=boat

NĀVĀSANA POSES

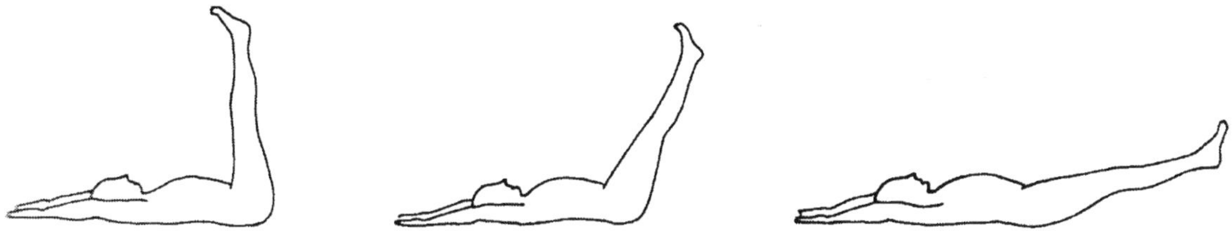

Ūrdhva Prasārita Pādāsana

Jaṭhara Parivartanāsana

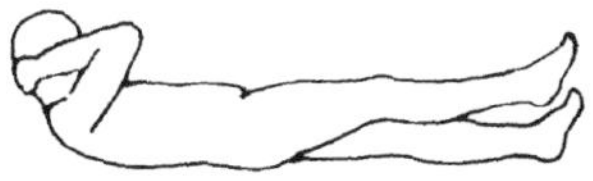

Eka Pāda Ardha Nāvāsana

Ardha Nāvāsana

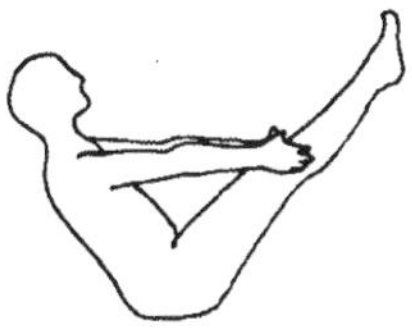

Paripūrṇa Nāvāsana

ŚĪRṢĀSANA CYCLE

1. **Sālamba Śīrṣāsana I** - 5-10 minutes
   sa=with; ālamba=support; śirṣa=head
2. **Parivṛtta Śīrṣāsana** - 1 minute
   parivṛtta=turned around
3. **Pārśva Eka Pāda Śīrṣāsana** - 30 seconds
   pārśva=sideways
4. **Eka Pāda Śīrṣāsana** - 30 seconds
   eka=one; pāda=leg, foot
5. **Vajra Śīrṣāsana** - 30 seconds
   vajra=thunderbolt, weapon of Indra
6. **Parivṛtta Vajra Śīrṣāsana** - 30 seconds
7. **Prasārita Pādottānāsana in Śīrṣāsana** - 1 minute
   prasārita=spread, extended; pāda=leg, foot; uttana=intense stretch
8. **Baddha Koṇāsana in Śīrṣāsana** - 1 minute
   baddha=bound; koṇa=angle

SARVĀNGĀSANA CYCLE

1. **Halāsana** - 4 minutes
   hala=plough
2. **Karṇapīdāsana** - 1 minute
   karṇa=ear; pīḍā=pressure
3. **Sālamba Sarvāngāsana I** - 10 minutes
   sa=with; ālamba=support; sarva=whole; anga=body
4. **Pārśva Eka Pāda Sarvāngāsana** - 30 seconds
   pārśva=sideways; eka=one; pāda=leg, foot
5. **Eka Pāda Sarvāngāsana** - 30 seconds
6. **Supta Koṇāsana** - 30 seconds
   supta=lying down; koṇa=angle
7. **Pārśva Halāsana** - 30 seconds
   pārśva=sideways; hala=plough
8. **Pārśva Karṇapīdāsana** - 30 seconds
   karṇa=ear; pīḍā=pressure
9. **Pārśva Sarvāngāsana**
10. **Pārśva Setu Bandha**
   setu=bridge; setu bandha=the construction of a bridge

ŚĪRṢĀSANA CYCLE

Sālamba Śīrṣāsana I

Parivṛtta Śīrṣāsana

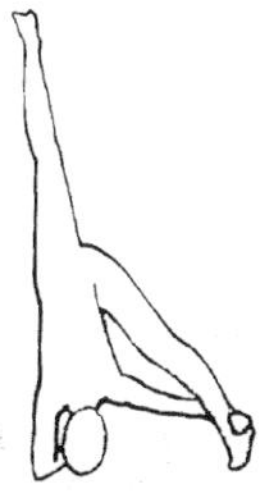

Pārśva Eka Pāda Śīrṣāsana

Eka Pāda Śīrṣāsana

Vajra Śīrṣāsana

Parivṛtta Vajra Śīrṣāsana

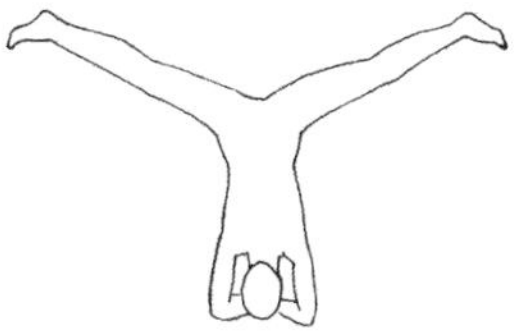

Prasārita Pādottānāsana in Śīrṣāsana

Baddha Koṇāsana in Śīrṣāsana

SARVĀNGĀSANA CYCLE

Halāsana

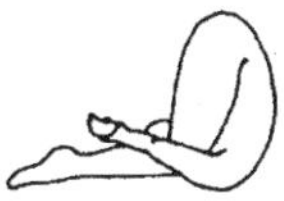

Karṇapīdāsana

Sālamba Sarvāngāsana I

Pārśva Eka Pāda Sarvāngāsana

Eka Pāda Sarvāngāsana

Supta Koṇāsana

Pārśva Halāsana

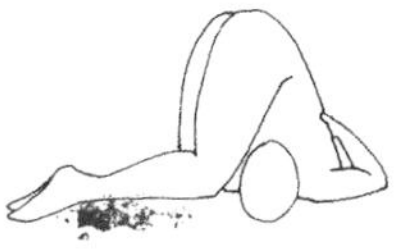

Pārśva Karṇapīdāsana

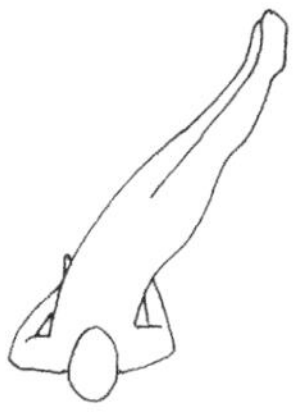

Pārśva Sarvāngāsana

Pārśva Setu Bandha

SITTING POSES

These Āsanas can be done in four different modes:

A. **Performing each pose separately,** and holding it for one minute. To release the knees you can do one minute of Paschimottānāsana between poses.

B. **Vinyasa I** - Connecting two or more poses by flowing from one into the other.

C. **Vinyasa II** - Interlacing all the poses with Sūrya Namaskar.

D. **Taking only the first pose of each series**, and holding it for five minutes each. Here too you can release the knees by doing one minute of Paschimottānāsana in between poses.

Finish the whole series off with 5-10 minutes Paschimottānāsana.

I - PADMĀSANA CYCLE - Short Timing

❖ **Change the crossing of the legs**

1. **Ardha Padmāsana** (half lotus) - 1 minute
   ardha=half; padma=lotus
2. **Padmāsana** - (All the following poses can be done in half lotus)
   a. **Padmāsana** - 1 minute
   b. **Parvatāsana** - 1 minute
   parvata=mountain
   b. **Gomukhāsana** - 1 minute
   go=cow; mukha=face
   c. **Namaste II** - 1 minute
3. **Yoga Mudrāsana I**
   mudra=closing, sealing
4. **Supta Padmāsana** - 1 minute
   supta=lying down; padma=lotus
5. **Matsyāsana I**
   matsya=fish
   a. **Matsyāsana I** - 1 minute
   b. **Paryankāsana I** - 30 seconds
   paryanka=couch
   c. **Paryankāsana II** - 30 seconds
6. **Matsyāsana II**
7. **Parivṛtta Padmāsana** - 1 minute
   parivṛtta=turned around

PADMĀSANA CYCLE

Ardha Padmāsana

Padmāsana

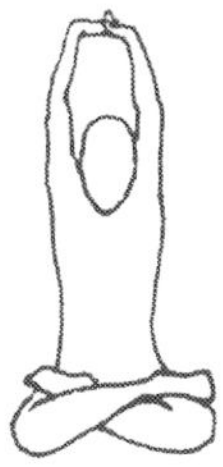
Parvatāsana

Gomukhāsana

Namaste II

Yoga Mudrāsana I

Supta Padmāsana

Matsyāsana I

Paryankāsana I

Paryankāsana II

Matsyāsana II

Parivṛtta Padmāsana

II - VAJRĀSANA CYCLE - Short Timing

1. **Vajrāsana I**
    a. **Vajrāsana I** - 1 minute
    vajra=thunderbolt, weapon of Indra
    b. **Parvatāsana** - 1 minute
    parvata=mountain
    c. **Gomukhāsana** - 1 minute
    go=cow; mukha=face
    d. **Namaste II** - 1 minute

2. **Vajrāsana II**

3. **Supta Vajrāsana**
    supta=lying down
    a. **Dwi Pāda Supta Vajrāsana** - 1 minute
    dwi=two; pāda=leg, foot
    b. **Eka Pāda Supta Vajrāsana** - 1 minute
    eka=one; pāda=leg, foot

III - VĪRĀSANA CYCLE - Short Timing

1. **Vīrāsana I**
    vīra=hero
    a. **Vīrāsana I** (knees together) - 1 minute
    b. **Parvatāsana** - 1 minute
    parvata=mountain
    c. **Gomukhāsana** - 1 minute
    go=cow; mukha=face
    d. **Namaste II** - 1 minute
    e. **Upaviṣṭha Vīrāsana I** (knees spread apart) - 1 minute

2. **Gomukhāsana** - full pose

3. **Supta Vīrāsana**
    a. **Eka Pāda Supta Vīrāsana** - 30 seconds
    eka=one; pāda=leg, foot
    b. **Paryankāsana I** - 30 seconds
    paryanka=couch
    c. **Paryankāsana II** - 30 seconds
    d. **Supta Vīrāsana** - 1 minute

4. **Bhekāsana**
    bheka=frog

VAJRĀSANA CYCLE

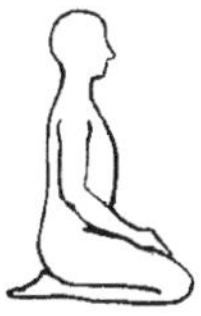
Vajrāsana I

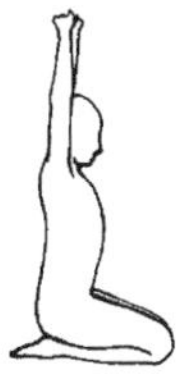
Parvatāsana

Gomukhāsana

Namaste II

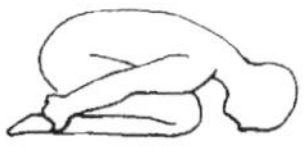
Vajrāsana II

Dwi Pāda Supta Vajrāsana

Eka Pāda Supta Vajrāsana

VĪRĀSANA CYCLE

Vīrāsana I

Parvatāsana

Gomukhāsana

Namaste II

Upaviṣṭha Vīrāsana I

Gomukhāsana
Full pose

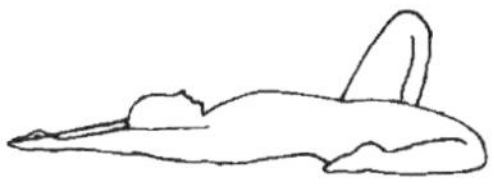
Eka Pāda Supta Vīrāsana

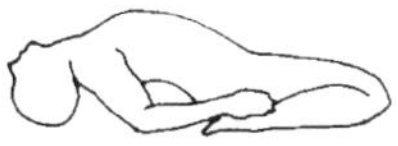
Paryankāsana I

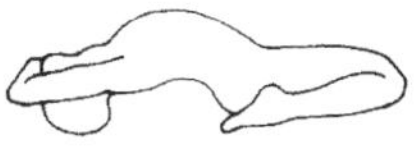
Paryankāsana II

Supta Vīrāsana

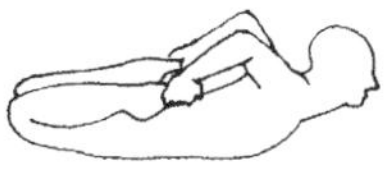
Bhekāsana

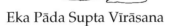

IV - BADDHA KOṆĀSANA CYCLE - Short Timing

1. **Baddha Koṇāsana I**
   a. **Baddha Koṇāsana I** - 1 minute
      baddha=bound; koṇa=angle
   b. **Parvatāsana** - 1 minute
      parvata=mountain
   c. **Gomukhāsana** - 1 minute
      go=cow; mukha=face
   d. **Namaste II** - 1 minute
2. **Supta Baddha Koṇāsana** - 1 minute
3. **Baddha Koṇāsana II** - 5 minutes

V - SITTING POSES - Long Timing, five minutes each pose

1. **Padmāsana**
2. **Yoga Mudrāsana I**
3. **Supta Padmāsana**
4. **Matsyāsana I**
5. **Matsyāsana II**
6. **Vajrāsana I**
7. **Vajrāsana II**
8. **Supta Vajrāsana**
9. **Vīrāsana I**
10. **Supta Vīrāsana**
11. **Baddha Koṇāsana II**
12. **Supta Baddha Koṇāsana**

LEG STRETCHES - Long Timing, five minutes each pose

1. **Ūrdhva Mukha Paschimottānāsana II**
   (legs together, holding feet with hands)
2. **Ūrdhva Mukha Prasārita Pādottānāsana II**
   (legs spread, holding feet with hands)
3. **Supta Pādānguṣṭhāsana I**
   (holding right leg with both hands)
4. **Supta Pādānguṣṭhāsana II**
   (with right hand bring right foot to right side)
5. **Supta Pādānguṣṭhāsana III**
   (with left hand bring right foot to left side)
6. **Repeat 3 through 5 with the left leg.**

BADDHA KOṆĀSANA CYCLE

Baddha Koṇāsana I

Parvatāsana

Gomukhāsana

Namaste II

Supta Baddha Koṇāsana

Baddha Koṇāsana II

SITTING POSES - LONG TIMIMG

Padmāsana

Yoga Mudrāsana I

Supta Padmāsana

Matsyāsana I

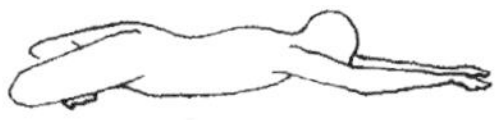
Matsyāsana II

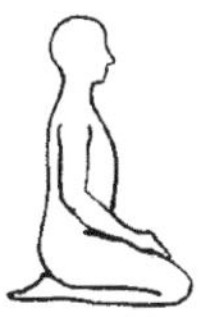
Vajrāsana I

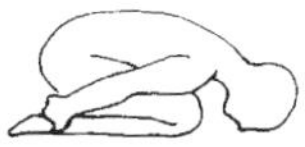
Vajrāsana II

Supta Vajrāsana

Vīrāsana I

Supta Vīrāsana

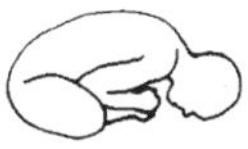
Baddha Koṇāsana II

Supta Baddha Koṇāsana

LEG STRECHES – LONG TIMING

Ūrdhva Mukha
Paschimottānāsana

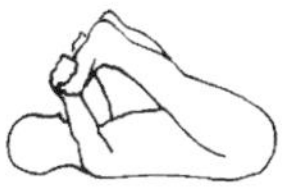
Ūrdhva Mukha
Prasārita Padottānāsana

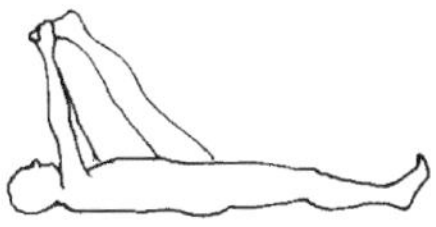
Supta Pādāngusṭhāsana I

Supta Pādāngusṭhāsana II

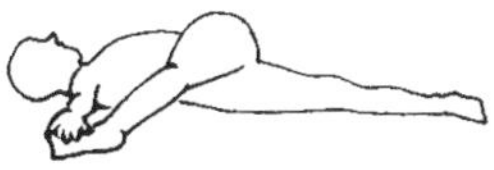
Supta Pādāngusṭhāsana III

Anantāsana

FULL PROGRAM

"This mighty energy is an equal and impartial mother, ***samam brahma***, in the great term of the Gita, and its intensity and force of movement is the same in the formation and the holding of a system of suns and the organization of the life of an ant-hill...

When we go behind and examine only the intensity of the movement of which quality and quantity are aspects, we realize that this Brahman dwells equally in all existences.

To Brahman there are no whole and parts, but each thing is all itself and benefits by the whole of Brahman.

Quality and quantity differ, the self is equal."

Śri Aurobindo - The Life Divine, pgs. 71-72

STANDING POSES - Full Program (Sunday)

These poses can be done in four different modes:

A. Performing each pose separately.
B. The Eight Forms (described in the intermediate program, p. 13).
C. Vinyasa I - Connecting two or more poses by flowing from one into the other.
D. Vinyasa II - Interlacing all the poses with Sūrya Namaskar.

The Poses:

1. **Tāḍāsana**
   tāḍa=mountain
2. **Utkaṭāsana**
   utkata=powerful,fierce
3. **Garuḍāsana** - 1 minute
   garuḍa=eagle
4. **Vṛkṣāsana I** - 1 minute
   vṛkṣa=tree
5. **Vṛkṣāsana II** - 1 minute

6. **Utthita Trikoṇāsana** - 1 minute
   utthita=extended; tri=three; koṇa=angle; trikoṇa=triangle
7. **Ardha Chandrāsana** - 1 minute
   ardha=half; chandra=moon
8. **Pārśvottānāsana** - 1 minute
   pārśva=side,flank; uttana=intense stretch
9. **Parivṛtta Trikoṇāsana** - 1 minute
   parivṛtta=turned around; trikoṇa=triangle
10. **Parivṛtta Ardha Chandrāsana** - 1 minute

11. **Vīrabhadrāsana II** - 1 minute
    Vīrabhadra is the name of a hero
12. **Utthita Pārśvakoṇāsana** - 1 minute
    utthita=extended; pārśva=sideways; koṇa=angle
13. **Parivṛtta Pārśvakoṇāsana** - 1 minute
    parivṛtta=turned around; pārśva=sideways; koṇa=angle
14. **Vīrabhadrāsana I** - 1 minute

15. **Vīrabhadrāsana III**

16. **Utthita Hasta Pādānguṣṭhāsana**
    utthita=extended; hasta=hand; pādānguṣṭha=big toe
    a. Holding the foot with the same side hand - 1 minute
    b. Holding the foot with the same side hand and bringing it to the side - 30 seconds
    c. Leg in the air

Tāḍāsana

Utkaṭāsana

Garuḍāsana

Vṛkṣāsana I

Vṛkṣāsana II

Utthita Trikoṇāsana

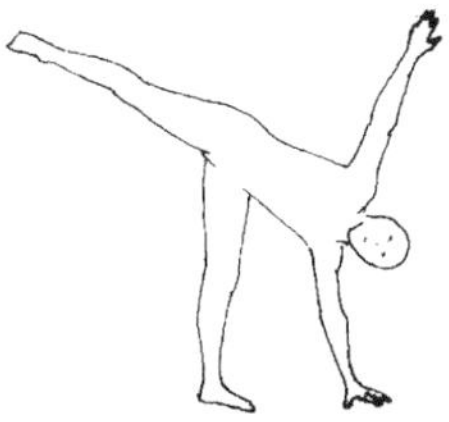
Ardha Chandrāsana

Pārśvottānāsana

Parivṛtta Trikoṇāsana

Parivṛtta Ardha Chandrāsana

Vīrabhadrāsana II

Utthita Pārśvakoṇāsana

Pārśvakoṇāsana

Vīrabhadrāsana I

Vīrabhadrāsana III

a b c
Utthita Hasta Pādānguṣṭhāsana

17. **Eka Pāda Uttānāsana** - 30 seconds
eka=one; pāda=leg, foot; uttana=intense stretch

18. **Prasārita Pādottānāsana** (three variations)
prasārita=spread, extended; pāda=leg, foot; uttana=intense stretch

19. **Uttānāsana**
uttana=intense stretch
   a. Catching big toe - 1 minute
   b. Palms under feet - 1 minute
   c. Holding ankles - 1 minute

FORWARD BENDS - Long Timing (Sunday, with standing poses)

It is possible to choose other poses from the forward bend series and alternate them with the poses presented here.

1. **Paschimottānāsana** - 10 minutes
paschima=the west, the back of the body; uttana=intense stretch

2. **Jānu Śīrṣāsana** - 5 minutes
jānu=knee; śirṣa=head

3. **Krounchāsana** - 5 minutes
krouncha=heron

4. **Upaviṣṭha Koṇāsana** - 5 minutes
pāda=leg, foot; upaviṣṭha=seated; koṇa=angle

5. **Baddha Koṇāsana II** - 5 minutes
baddha=bound; koṇa=angle

6. **Kūrmāsana** - 5 minutes
kūrma=tortoise

7. **Eka Pāda Śīrṣāsana** - 1 minute
eka=one; pāda=leg, foot; śirṣa=head

8. **Yoganidrāsana** - 1 minute
nidrā=sleep

9. **Dwi Pāda Śīrṣāsana**
dwi=two; pāda=leg, foot; śirṣa=head

10. **Parivṛtta Padmāsana** - 1 minute
parvritta=turned around; padma=lotus

~ **Śavāsana** ~

Eka Pāda Uttānāsana

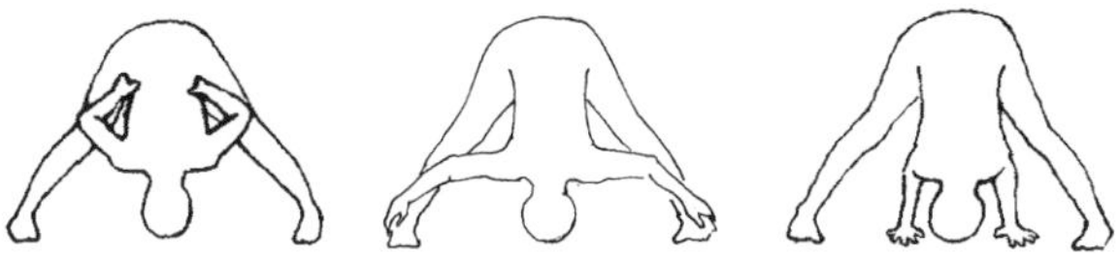

Prasārita Pādottānāsana

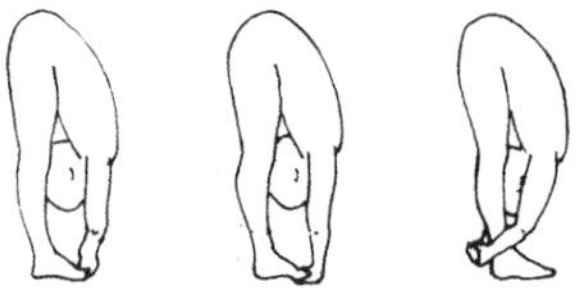

Uttānāsana

FORWARD BENDS – LONG TIMING

Paschimottānāsana

Jānu Śīrṣāsana

Krounchāsana

Upaviṣṭha Koṇāsana

Baddha Koṇāsana II

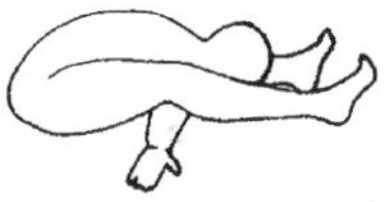

Kūrmāsana

Eka Pāda Śīrṣāsana

Yoganidrāsana

Dwi Pāda Śīrṣāsana

Parivṛtta Padmāsana

HAND BALANCES - Full Program (Monday, Friday)

These poses can be done in four different modes:

- **A.** **Performing each pose separately,** and holding it for thirty seconds.
- **B.** **Vinyasa I** - Connecting two or more poses by flowing from one into the other.
- **C.** **Vinyasa II** - Interlacing all the poses with Sūrya Namaskar,
- **D.** **You can start poses 17 through 26,** each from Sālamba Śīrṣāsana II, finishing it with going back and pushing up into Ūrdhva Dhanurāsana.

The Poses:

1. **Adho Mukha Vṛkṣāsana** - 1 minute
   adho=downwards; mukha=face; vṛkṣa=tree
2. **Padma Adho Mukha Vṛkṣāsana** - 30 seconds
   padma=lotus
3. **Pīncha Mayūrāsana** - 1 minute
   pincha=chin, feather; mayūra=peacock
4. **Padma Pīncha Mayūrāsana** - 30 seconds
   padma=lotus
5. **Vasiṣṭhāsana I** - 30 seconds
   Vasiṣṭha is the name of a sage
6. **Vasiṣṭhāsana II** - 30 seconds
7. **Kaśyapāsana** - 30 seconds
   Kaśyapa is the son of Marīchi
8. **Viśvāmitrāsana** - 30 seconds
   Viśvāmitra is the name of a sage
9. **Dwi Hasta Bhujāsana** - 30 seconds
   dwi=two; hasta=hand; bhuja=arm
10. **Tittibhāsana** - 30 seconds
    tittibha=firefly
11. **Bhujapidāsana** - 30 seconds
    bhuja=arm; pīḍā=pressure
12. **Eka Hasta Bhujāsana**
    eka=one; hasta=hand; bhuja=arm
13. **Aṣṭāvakrāsana**
    Aṣṭāvakra is the teacher of King Janaka
14. **Mayūrāsana**
    mayūra=peacock
15. **Padma Mayūrāsana**
    padma=lotus
16. **Haṃsāsana**
    haṃsa=swan
17. **Bakāsana**
    baka=crane
18. **Pārśva Bakāsana**
    pārśva=sideways

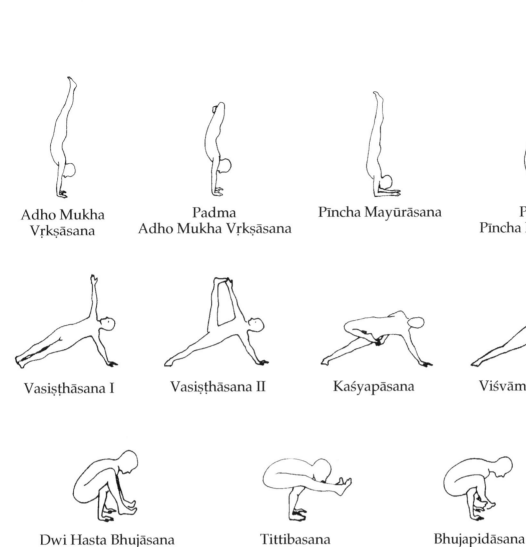

Adho Mukha
Vṛkṣāsana

Padma
Adho Mukha Vṛkṣāsana

Pīncha Mayūrāsana

Padma
Pīncha Mayūrāsana

Vasiṣṭhāsana I

Vasiṣṭhāsana II

Kaśyapāsana

Viśvāmitrāsana

Dwi Hasta Bhujāsana

Tittibasana

Bhujapidāsana

Eka Hasta Bhujāsana

Aṣṭāvakrāsana

Mayūrāsana

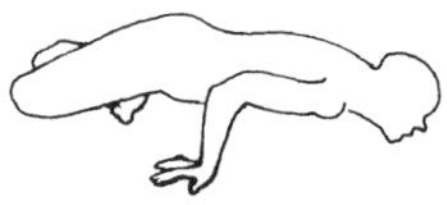

Padma Mayūrāsana

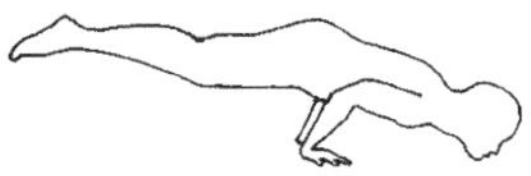

Hamsāsana

Bakāsana

Pārśva Bakāsana

19. **Eka Pāda Bakāsana I**
eka=one; pāda=leg, foot
20. **Eka Pāda Bakāsana II**
21. **Dwi Pāda Kouṇḍinyāsana**
dwi=two; pāda=leg, foot; Kouṇḍinya is the name of a sage.
22. **Eka Pāda Kouṇḍinyāsana**
eka=one; pāda=leg, foot
23. **Eka Pāda Gālavāsana**
Gālava is the name of a sage
24. **Ūrdhva Kukkuṭāsana**
ūrdhva=upwards; kukkuṭa=cock
25. **Gālavāsana**
26. **Pārśva Kukkuṭāsana**
pārśva=sideways

Paschimottānāsana - 10-20 minutes

~ Śavāsana ~

Eka Pāda Bakāsana I

Eka Pāda Bakāsana II

Dwi Pāda Kouṇḍinyāsana

Eka Pāda Kouṇḍinyāsana

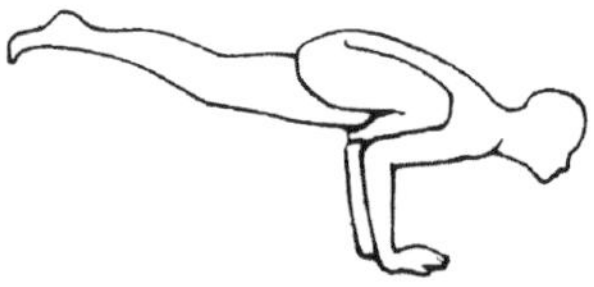

Eka Pāda Gālavāsana

Ūrdhva Kukkuṭāsana

Gālavāsana

Pārśva Kukkuṭāsana

Paschimottānāsana

SIMPLE BACKBENDS - Full Program (Tuesday)

(Optional, as some practice on this day the backbend variations - p. 38)

These poses can be done in three different modes:

A. Performing each pose separately.
B. Vinyasa I - Connecting two or more poses by flowing from one into the other.
C. Vinyasa II - Interlacing all the poses with Sūrya Namaskar.

The Poses:

1. **Adho Mukha Śvānāsana** - 1 minute
2. **Adho Mukha Vṛkṣāsana** - 1 minute
3. **Pīncha Mayūrāsana** - 1 minute
4. **Eka Pāda Śalabhāsana**
   eka=one; pāda=leg, foot
   a. Arms forwards, same side arm and leg up x3
   b. Arms forwards, opposite arm and leg up x3
5. **Ūrdhva Mukha Śalabhāsana**
   ūrdhva=upwards; mukha=face; salabha=locust
   a. Arms backwards x3
   b. Arms sideways x3
   c. Arms forwards x3
   d. Makarāsana x3
   makara=crocodile
6. **Dwi Pāda Śalabhāsana**
   dwi=two; pāda=leg, foot
   a. Head and arms on the ground x3
   b. Arms backwards x3
   c. Arms sideways x3
   d. Arms forwards x3
   e. Makarāsana x3
   makara=crocodile
7. **Dhanurāsana**
   dhanu=bow
8. **Bhujaṅgāsana**
   bhujaṅga=serpent
9. **Ūrdhva Mukha Śvānāsana**
   ūrdhva=upwards; mukha=face; ṣvāna=dog
10. **Uṣṭrāsana**
    uṣṭra=camel
11. **Setu Bandha** - 1-5 minutes
12. **Eka Pāda Setu Bandha**
    eka=one; pāda=leg, foot

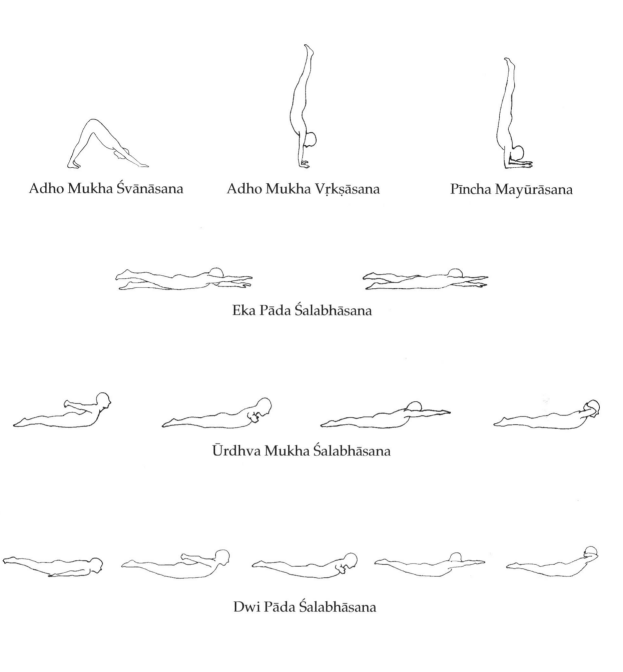

Adho Mukha Śvānāsana

Adho Mukha Vṛkṣāsana

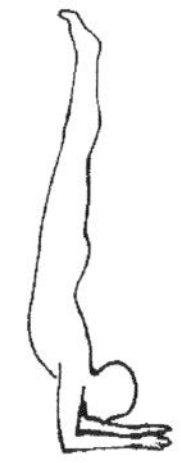

Pīncha Mayūrāsana

Eka Pāda Śalabhāsana

Ūrdhva Mukha Śalabhāsana

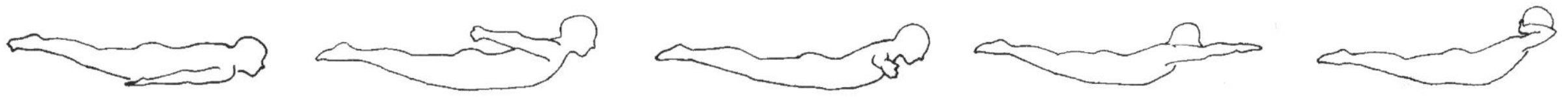

Dwi Pāda Śalabhāsana

Dhanurāsana

Bhujaṇgāsana

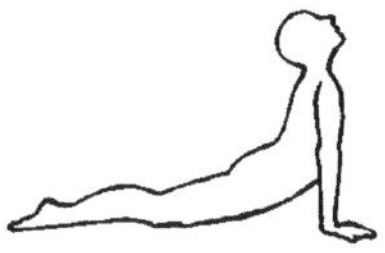

Ūrdhva Mukha Śvānāsana

Uṣṭrāsana

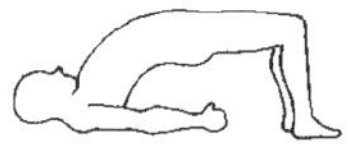

Setu Bandha

Eka Pāda Setu Bandha

13. Eka Pāda Rājakapotāsana I
(one leg in Jānu Śīrṣāsana)
eka=one; pāda=leg, foot; rāja-kapota=king of the pigeons

14. Eka Pāda Rājakapotāsana II
(balancing on one foot and one knee)

15. Eka Pāda Rājakapotāsana III
(one leg in Vīrāsana)

16. Eka Pāda Rājakapotāsana IV
a. Hanumānāsana
b. Eka Pāda Rājakapotāsana IV

Leg Stretches - Short Timing (Tuesday, Thursday, Saturday)

1. Ūrdhva Mukha Paschimottānāsana II - 1 minute
(legs together, holding feet with hands)
ūrdhva=upwards; mukha=face; paschima=the west, the back of the body; uttana=intense stretch

2. Ūrdhva Mukha Prasārita Pādottānāsana II - 1 minute
(legs spread, holding feet with hands)
prasārita=extended; pāda=leg, foot; uttana=intense stretch

3. Supta Pādānguṣṭhāsana I - 1 minute
(holding right leg with both hands)
supta=lying down; pādāṅguṣṭha=big toe

4. Supta Pādānguṣṭhāsana II - 1 minute
(with right hand bring right foot to right side)

5. Supta Pādānguṣṭhāsana III
(with left hand bring right foot to left side) - 1 minute

6. Anantāsana - 1 minute
ananta=infinite

7. Repeat 3 through 6 with the left leg.

~ Śavāsana ~

Eka Pāda
Rājakapotāsana I

Eka Pāda
Rājakapotāsana II

Eka Pāda
Rājakapotāsana III

Hanumānāsana

Eka Pāda Rājakapotāsana IV

LEG STRECHES

Ūrdhva Mukha
Paschimottānāsana II

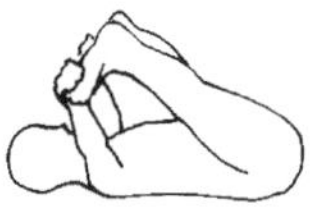

Ūrdhva Mukha
Prasārita Padottānāsana II

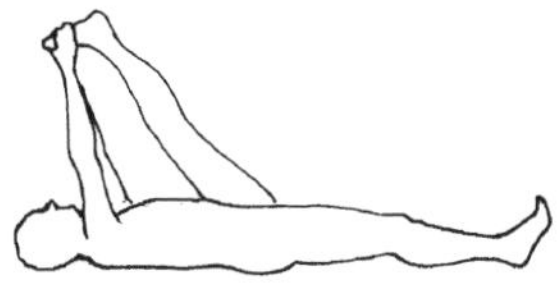

Supta Pādānguṣṭhāsana I

Supta Pādānguṣṭhāsana II

Supta Pādānguṣṭhāsana III

Anantāsana

FORWARD BENDS - Short Timing, Full Program (Wednesday)

These poses can be done in four different modes:

A. **Performing each pose separately,** and holding it for one minute.
B. **Vinyasa I** - Connecting two or more poses by flowing from one into the other.
C. **Vinyasa II** - Interlacing all the poses with Sūrya Namaskar, and holding each forward bend for one minute.
D. **Vinyasa III** - A variation of Vinyasa I & II in which the twists are included.

The Poses:

1. **Paschimottānāsana** - 10 minutes
   paschima=the west, the back of the body; uttana=intense stretch
2. **Parivṛtta Paschimottānāsana** - 1 minute
   parivṛtta=turned around
3. **Jānu Śīrṣāsana**
   twisting and elongating upwards - 1 minute
   coming forwards - 1 minute
   jānu=knee; śirṣa=head
4. **Parivṛtta Jānu Śīrṣāsana**
   twisting and elongating upwards - 1 minute
   turning - 1 minute
   parivṛtta=turned around
5. **Ardha Baddha Padma Paschimottānāsana**
   twisting and elongating upwards - 1 minute
   coming forwards - 1 minute
   ardha=half; baddha=bound; padma=lotus
6. **Triang Mukhaikapāda Paschimottānāsana**
   twisting and elongating upwards - 1 minute
   coming forwards - 1 minute
   tri=three; anga=limb; mukha=face; eka=one; pāda=foot
7. **Krounchāsana**
   elongating upwards - 1 minute
   head towards shin - 1 minute
   krouncha=heron
8. **Ākarṇa Dhanurāsana**
   a=near to; karṇa=ear; dhanu=bow
9. **Marīchyāsana I**
   twisting and elongating upwards - 1 minute
   coming forwards - 1 minute
10. **Marīchyāsana II**
    twisting and elongating - 1 minute
    coming forwards - 1 minute

Paschimottānāsana

Parivṛtta Paschimottānāsana

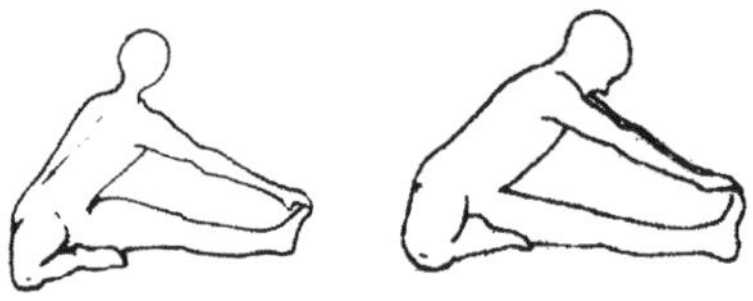
Jānu Śīrṣāsana

Parivṛtta
Jānu Śīrṣāsana

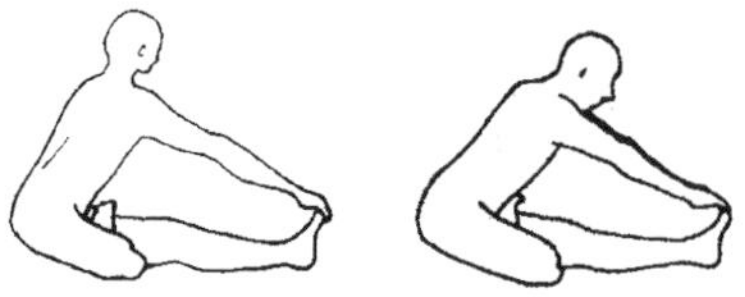
Ardha Baddha Padma
Paschimottānāsana

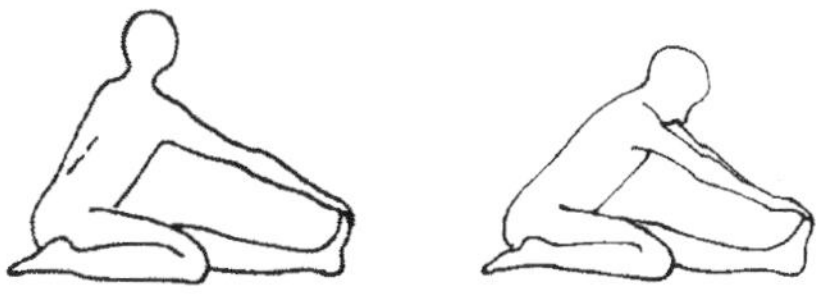
Triang Mukhaikapāda
Paschimottānāsana

Krounchāsana

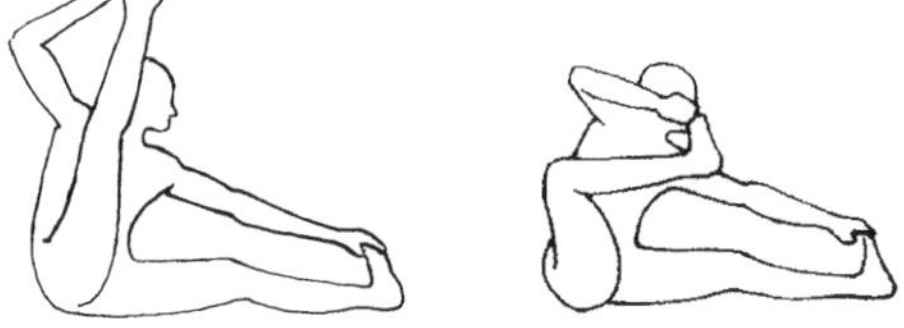
Ākarṇa Dhanurāsana

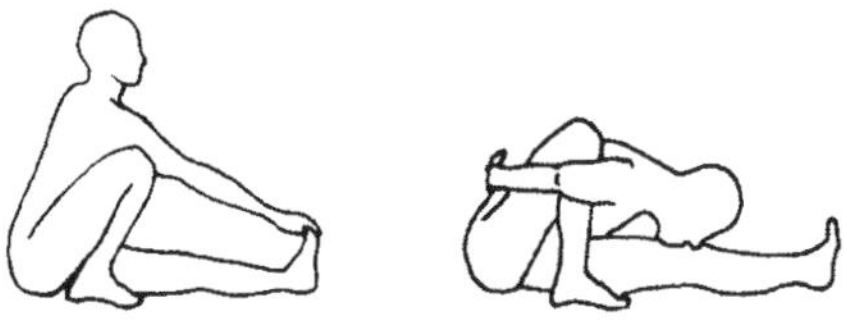
Marīchyāsana I

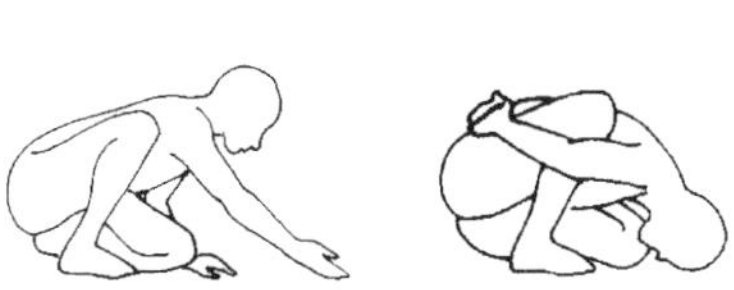
Marīchyāsana II

11. Ubhaya Pādānguṣṭhāsana
ubhaya=both; pādāṅguṣṭha=big toe
- **a. Ubhaya Pādānguṣṭhāsana** - 1 minute
- **b. Ūrdhva Mukha Prasārita Pādottānāsana I** - 1 minute
  ūrdhva=upwards; mukha=face; prasārita=spread; pāda=leg, foot; uttana=intense stretch

12. Ūrdhva Mukha Paschimottānāsana I - 1 minute
paschima=the west, the back of the body

13. Upaviṣṭha Koṇāsana - 5 minutes
upaviṣṭha=seated; koṇa=angle

14. Baddha Koṇāsana II - 5 minutes
baddha=bound; koṇa=angle

15. Mālāsana (clasping the hands on the back) - 1 minute
mālā=garland

16. Kūrmāsana - 1 minute
kūrma=tortoise

17. Eka Pāda Śīrṣāsana - 1 minute
eka=one; pāda=leg, foot; śirṣa=head

18. Bhairavāsana (lying on the back) - 1 minute
bhairava=terrible, formidable

19. Skandāsana (sitting and bending forward)
Skanda is Kārtikeya, the god of war

20. Chakorāsana (balancing on both hands)
chakora is a bird

21. Kāla Bhairavāsana (balancing on one hand and one foot)
Kāla-Bhairava is Śiva in his terrible aspect as destroyer of the universe

22. Dūrvāsāsana (standing on one foot)
Durvāsā is the name of a saint

23. Ruchikāsana (standing on one foot and bending forward)
Ruchika is the name of a sage

24. Yoganidrāsana - 1 minute
nidrā=sleep

25. Dwi Pāda Śīrṣāsana
dwi=two; pāda=leg, foot; śirṣa=head
- **a. Dwi Pāda Śīrṣāsana I** - 1 minute
- **b. Dwi Pāda Śīrṣāsana II** (balancing on both hands)
- **c. Tittibhāsana**
  tittibha=firefly

Ubhaya Pādānguṣṭhāsana

Ūrdhva Mukha
Prasārita Pādottānāsana I

Ūrdhva Mukha
Paschimottānāsana I

Upaviṣṭha Koṇāsana

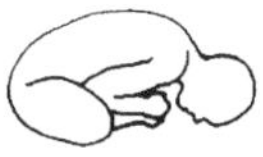

Baddha Koṇāsana II

Mālāsana

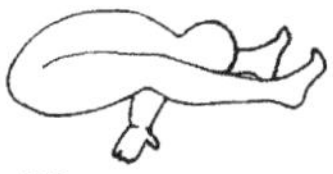

Kūrmāsana

Eka Pāda Śīrṣāsana

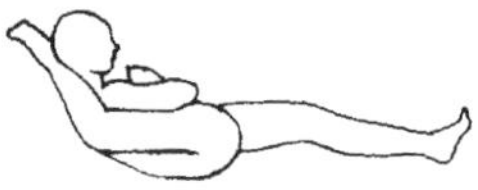

Bhairavāsana

Skandāsana

Chakorāsana

Kāla Bhairavāsana

Dūrvāsāsana

Ruchikāsana

Yoganidrāsana

Dwi Pāda Śīrṣāsana I

Dwi Pāda Śīrṣāsana II

Tittibhāsana

TWISTS - Full Program (Wednesday, together with forward bends)

1. **Parivṛtta Eka Pāda Padmāsana I** - 1 minute
   (one leg straight, holding the Padmāsana foot)
   parvritta=turned around; eka=one; pāda=leg, foot; padma=lotus
2. **Parivṛtta Eka Pāda Padmāsana II** - 1 minute
   (one leg straight, holding the Padmāsana shin)
3. **Parivṛtta Padmāsana** - 1 minute
4. **Bharadvājāsana I** (holding the arm) - 1 minute
   Bharadvāja is the father of Drona
5. **Bharadvājāsana II** (holding the Padmāsana foot) - 1 minute
6. **Vāmadevāsana**
   Vāmadeva is the name of a sage
7. **Yogadaṇḍāsana**
   daṇḍa=staff
8. **Marīchyāsana III** (one leg straight) - 1 minute
   Marīchi is a sage.
9. **Marīchyāsana IV** (one leg in Vīrāsana) - 1 minute
10. **Marīchyāsana V** (one leg in Padmāsana)
11. **Pāśāsana** - 30 seconds
    pāśa=noose, cord
12. **Ardha Matsyendrāsana** - 1 minute
    ardha=half; matsya=fish; indra=king;
    Matsyendra is one of the founders of Haṭha Vidyā

VINYASA III - A variation of Vinyasa I & II in which the forward bends and twists are combined.

1. **Sūrya Namaskar I** 3x
2. **Uttānāsana** (3 variations)
3. **Paschimottānāsana**
   (Daṇḍāsana + 3 variations) - 7 minutes
   Pūrvottānāsana
4. **Jānu Śīrṣāsana**
   twisting and elongating upwards - 1 minute
   coming forwards - 1 minute
   Parivṛtta Jānu Śīrṣāsana - 1 minute
5. **Ardha Baddha Padma Paschimottānāsana**
   twisting and elongating upwards - 1 minute
   coming forwards - 1 minute
   Parivṛtta Eka Pāda Padmāsana - 1 minute

TWISTS

Parivṛtta Eka Pāda Padmāsana I

Parivṛtta Eka Pāda Padmāsana II

Parivṛtta Padmāsana

Bharadvājāsana I

Bharadvājāsana II

Vāmadevāsana

Yogadaṇḍāsana

Marīchyāsana III

Marīchyāsana IV

Marīchyāsana V

Pāśāsana

Ardha Matsyendrāsana

VINYASA III

Sūrya Namaskar

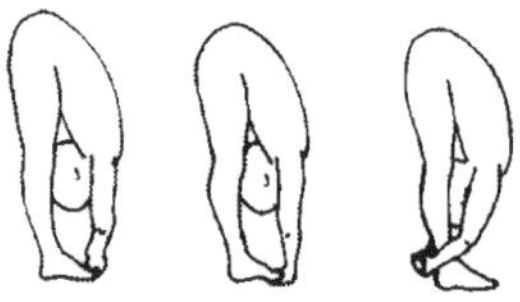

Uttānāsana

Daṇḍāsana

Paschimottānāsana

Pūrvottānāsana

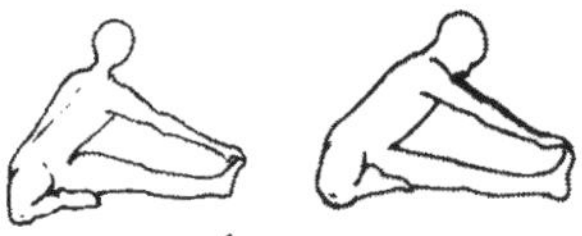

Jānu Śīrṣāsana

Parivṛtta Jānu Śīrṣāsana

Ardha Baddha Padma Paschimottānāsana

Parivṛtta Eka Pāda Padmāsana

6. **Triang Mukhaikapāda Paschimottānāsana**
   twisting and elongating upwards - 1 minute
   coming forwards - 1 minute
   Marīchyāsana IV - 1 minute
7. **Krounchāsana**
   elongating upwards - 1 minute
   head towards shin - 1 minute
   Bharadvājāsana II - 1 minute
8. **Marīchyāsana I**
   twisting and elongating upwards - 1 minute
   coming forwards - 1 minute
   Marīchyāsana III - 1 minute
9. **Marīchyāsana II**
   elongating upwards - 1 minute
   coming forwards - 1 minute
   Marīchyāsana V - 1 minute
10. **Ubhaya Pādānguṣṭhāsana**
    Ubhaya Pādānguṣṭhāsana - 1 minute
    Ūrdhva Mukha Prasārita Pādottānāsana I - 1 minute
11. **Upaviṣṭha Koṇāsana**
    elongating upwards - 1 minute
    coming forwards - 4 minutes
    Vāmadevāsana
    Yogadaṇḍāsana
12. **Baddha Koṇāsana**
    elongating upwards - 1 minute
    coming forwards - 4 minutes
    Mūlabhandāsana - 1 minute
    Kandāsana - 1 minute
13. **Mālāsana**
    Mālāsana - 1 minute
    Pāśāsana - 1 minute
14. **Kūrmāsana** - 1 minute
15. **Ākarṇa Dhanurāsana**
16. **Eka Pāda Śīrṣāsana**
17. **Yoganidrāsana** - 1 minute
18. **Ardha Matsyendrāsana** - 1 minute
19. **Parivṛtta Padmāsana** - 1 minute

~ Śavāsana ~

Triang Mukhaikapāda
Paschimottānāsana

Marīchyāsana IV

Krounchāsana

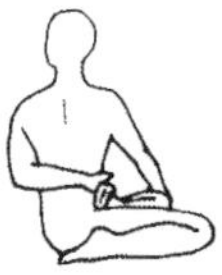

Bharadvājāsana II

Marīchyāsana I

Marīchyāsana III

Marīchyāsana II

Marīchyāsana V

Ubhaya
Pādāngusṭhāsana

Ūrdhva Mukha
Prasārita Pādottānāsana I

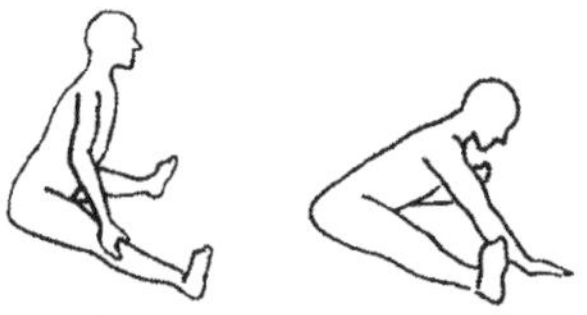

Upaviṣṭha Koṇāsana

Vāmadevāsana

Yogadaṇḍāsana

Baddha Koṇāsana

Mūlabhandāsana

Kandāsana

Mālāsana

Pāśāsana

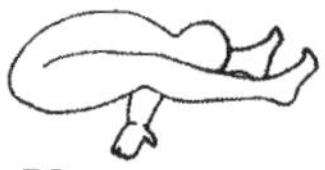

Kūrmāsana

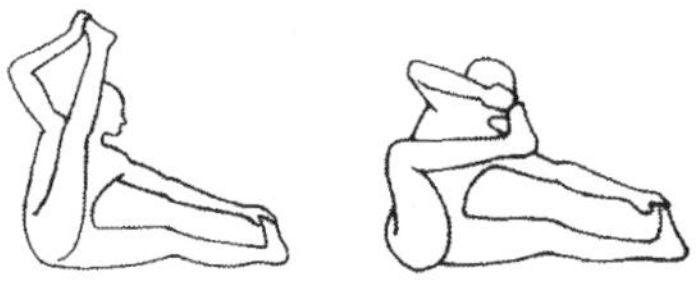

Ākarṇa Dhanurāsana

Eka Pāda Sirsasana

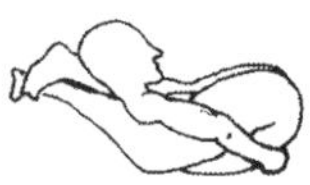

Yoganidrāsana

Ardha Matsyendrāsana

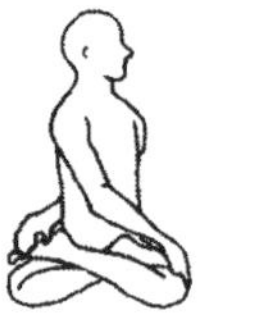

Parivṛtta Padmāsana

STANDING POSES & ŪRDHVA DHANURĀSANA x 108

(Thursday)

These poses can be done in four different modes:

A. Performing standing poses and then and then a few Ūrdhva Dhanurāsanas to the wall.
B. Repeating Sūrya Namaskar x 54 up to 108
C. 108 Ūrdhva Dhanurāsanas, as follows:

1. **Sūrya Namaskar** - x3
   adho=downwards; mukha=face; ṣvāna=dog
2. **Adho Mukha Vṛkṣāsana** - 1 minute
   adho=downwards; mukha=face; vṛkṣa=tree
3. **Pīncha Mayūrāsana** - 1 minute
   pincha=chin, feather; mayūra= peacock
4. **Ūrdhva Dhanurāsana** - x108
   ūrdhva=upwards; dhanu=bow
5. **Uttānāsana** - 5 minutes
   uttana=intense stretch
6. **Leg Stretches**
   a. Ūrdhva Mukha Paschimottānāsana II - 1 minute
   b. Ūrdhva Mukha Prasārita Pādottānāsana II - 1 minute
   c. Supta Pādānguṣṭhāsana I - 1 minute
   d. Supta Pādānguṣṭhāsana II - 1 minute
   e. Supta Pādānguṣṭhāsana III - 1 minute
   f. Anantāsana - 1 minute
   g. Repeat c. through f. with the left leg.

~ Śavāsana ~

Sūrya Namaskar I

Adho Mukha Vṛkṣāsana

Pīncha Mayūrāsana

Ūrdhva Dhanurāsana

Uttānāsana

Ūrdhva Mukha
Paschimottānāsana II

Ūrdhva Mukha
Prasārita Padottānāsana II

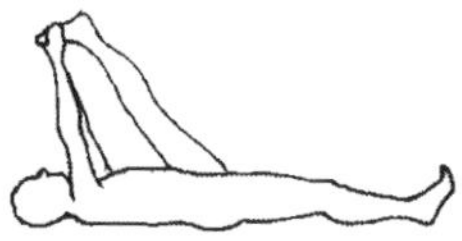

Supta Pādānguṣṭhāsana I

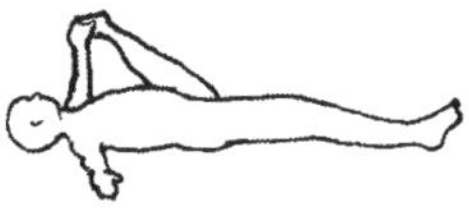

Supta Pādānguṣṭhāsana II

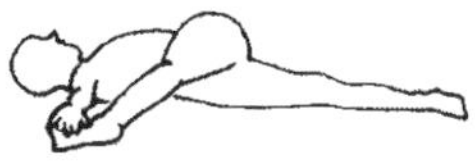

Supta Pādānguṣṭhāsana III

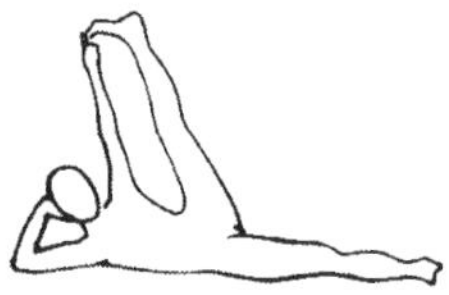

Anantāsana

BACKBEND VARIATIONS - Full Program (Tuesday, Saturday)

These poses can be done in three different modes:

A. Performing each pose separately, and holding it for thirty seconds.

B. Vinyasa I - Connecting two or more poses by flowing from one into the other.

C. Vinyasa II - Interlacing all the poses with Sūrya Namaskar.

The Poses:

1. **Adho Mukha Śvānāsana** - 1 minute
   adho=downwards; mukha=face; ṣvāna=dog
2. **Adho Mukha Vṛkṣāsana** - 1 minute
   adho=downwards; mukha=face; vṛkṣa=tree
3. **Pīncha Mayūrāsana** - 1 minute
   pincha=chin, feather; mayūra=peacock

Śīrṣāsana I, going back to Viparīta Daṇḍāsana and going into each pose:

4. **Ūrdhva Dhanurāsana**
   ūrdhva=upwards; dhanu=bow
5. **Eka Pāda Ūrdhva Dhanurāsana**
   eka=one; pāda=leg, foot
6. **Dwi Pāda Viparīta Daṇḍāsana**
   dwi=two; pāda=leg, foot; viparīta=reverse; daṇḍa=staff
7. **Eka Pāda Viparīta Daṇḍāsana I**
   eka=one; pāda=leg, foot
8. **Maṇḍalāsana**
   maṇḍala=circle
9. **Chakra Bandhāsana**
   chakra=wheel; bandha=bound
10. **Eka Pāda Viparīta Daṇḍāsana II**
11. **Vṛśchikāsana I** (from Adho Mukha Vṛkṣāsana)
    vṛśchika=scorpion
12. **Vṛśchikāsana II** (from Pīncha Mayūrāsana)
13. **Kapotasāna** - 1 minute
    kapota=pigeon.
14. **Laghuvajrāsana**
    laghu=small, beautiful; vajra=thunderbolt
15. **Pādāṅguṣṭha Dhanurāsana**
    pādāṅguṣṭha=big toe; dhanu=bow
    a. **Pādāṅguṣṭha Dhanurāsana I** (feet high)
    b. **Pādāṅguṣṭha Dhanurāsana II** (feet on head)
16. **Rājakapotāsana**
    (legs bent, hands on earth, head on feet)

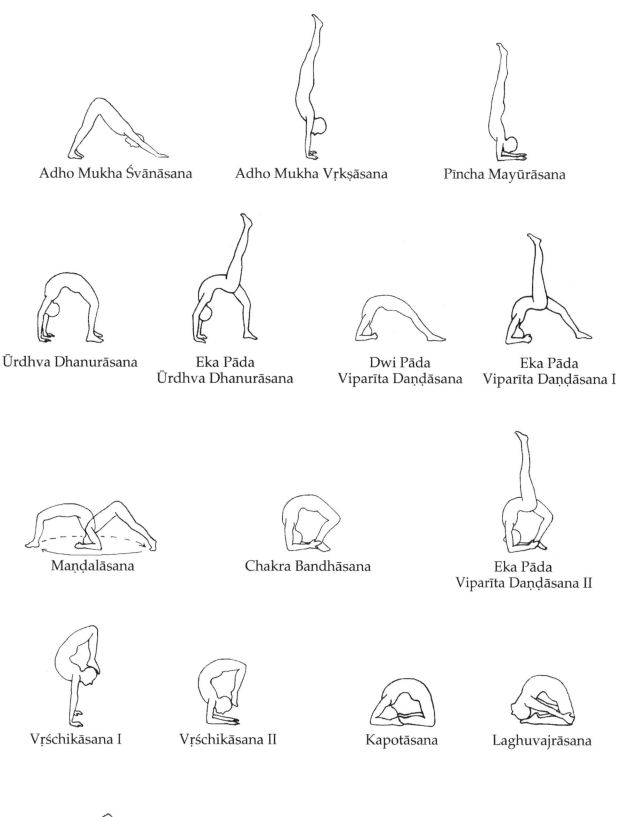

Adho Mukha Śvānāsana

Adho Mukha Vṛkṣāsana

Pīncha Mayūrāsana

Ūrdhva Dhanurāsana

Eka Pāda Ūrdhva Dhanurāsana

Dwi Pāda Viparīta Daṇḍāsana

Eka Pāda Viparīta Daṇḍāsana I

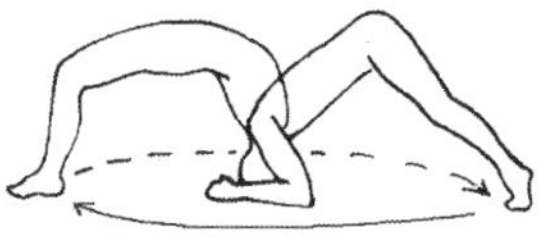
Maṇḍalāsana

Chakra Bandhāsana

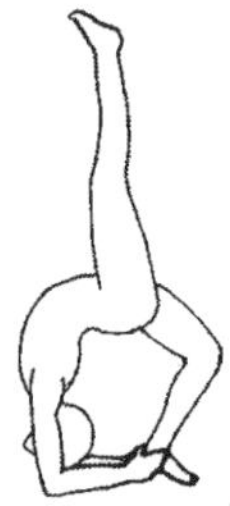
Eka Pāda Viparīta Daṇḍāsana II

Vṛśchikāsana I

Vṛśchikāsana II

Kapotāsana

Laghuvajrāsana

Pādāṅguṣṭha Dhanurāsana I

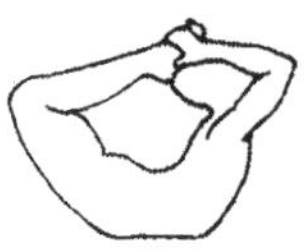
Pādāṅguṣṭha Dhanurāsana II

Rājakapotāsana

17. Gheraṇḍāsana
(a combination of Bhekāsana and Pādāṅguṣṭha Dhanurāsana)
Gheraṇḍa is the name of a sage, author of the Gheraṇḍa Saṁhitā

18. Kapiṅjalāsana
(a combination of Vasiṣṭhāsana and Pādāṅguṣṭha Dhanurāsana)
Kapiṅjalna is a kind of partridge

19. Gaṇḍa Bheruṇḍāsana
gaṇḍa=cheek; bheruṇḍna=terrible, formidable;
gaṇḍa-bheruṇḍa is a species of bird

20. Eka Pāda Rājakapotāsana I
(one leg in Jānu Śīrṣāsana)
eka=one; pāda=leg, foot; rāja-kapota=king of the pigeons

21. Eka Pāda Rājakapotāsana II
(balancing on one foot and one knee)

22. Eka Pāda Rājakapotāsana III
(one leg in Vīrāsana)

23. Eka Pāda Rājakapotāsana IV
a. Hanumānāsana
b. Eka Pāda Rājakapotāsana IV

24. Naṭarājāsana
naṭa=dance; rāja=king; Naṭarāja is a name of Śiva, lord of dance and destruction (the Tāṇḍava is the dance of destruction)
- **a. Naṭarājāsana I** (foot high)
- **b. Naṭarājāsana II** (foot on head)

25. Tiriang Mukhottānāsana
tiring=reverse, upside down; mukha=face; uttana=intense stretch

26. Uttānāsana - 5 minutes
uttana=intense stretch.

Leg Stretches - Short Timing (Tuesday, Thursday and Saturday)

1. **Ūrdhva Mukha Paschimottānāsana II** (legs together) - 1 minute
2. **Ūrdhva Mukha Prasārita Pādottānāsana II** (legs spread) - 1 minute
3. **Supta Pādānguṣṭhāsana I** - 1 minute
(holding right leg with both hands)
4. **Supta Pādānguṣṭhāsana II** - 1 minute
(with right hand bring right foot to right side)
5. **Supta Pādānguṣṭhāsana III** - 1 minute
(with left hand bring right foot to left side)
6. **Anantāsana** - 1 minute
7. **Repeat 3 through 6 with the left leg.**

~ Śavāsana ~

Gheraṇḍāsana

Kapiñjalāsana

Gaṇḍa Bheruṇḍāsana

Eka Pāda
Rājakapotāsana I

Eka Pāda
Rājakapotāsana II

Eka Pāda
Rājakapotāsana III

Hanumānāsana

Eka Pāda Rājakapotāsana IV

Naṭarājāsana I

Naṭarājāsana II

Tiriang Mukhottānāsana

Uttānāsana

LEG STRECHES

Ūrdhva Mukha
Paschimottānāsana II

Ūrdhva Mukha
Prasārita Padottānāsana II

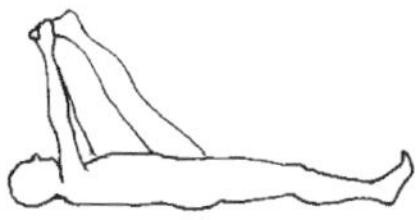

Supta Pādānguṣṭhāsana I

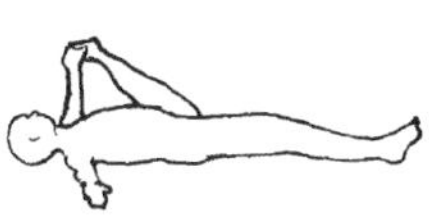

Supta Pādānguṣṭhāsana II

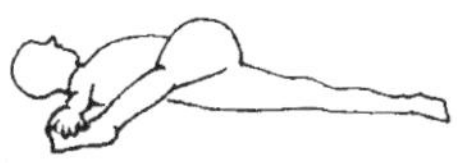

Supta Pādānguṣṭhāsana III

Anantāsana

AFTERNOON PRACTICE - Full Program

The daily afternoon practice includes Nāvāsana poses, the head and shoulder stand cycles and one group of sitting poses. If performed fully it will take approximately 1½ hours.

Women should avoid headstand and shoulder stand during their menstrual period.

NĀVĀSANA POSES

1. **Ūrdhva Prasārita Pādāsana** - x3
   holding the legs for 30 seconds at 90 degrees, then for 15 seconds at 60 and 30 degrees respectfully
   ūrdhva=upwards; prasārita=extended; pāda=leg, foot

2. **Jaṭhara Parivartanāsana** - 5 times to each side
   jaṭhara=stomach; parivartana=turning, rolling.

3. **Nāvāsanas**
   - A. **Ardha Nāvāsana**
     1. **Eka Pāda Ardha Nāvāsana** - x2
     2. **Ardha Nāvāsana** - x2
   - B. **Paripūrṇa Nāvāsana** - x2
     ardha=half; paripūrṇa=full; nāva=boat

NĀVĀSANA POSES

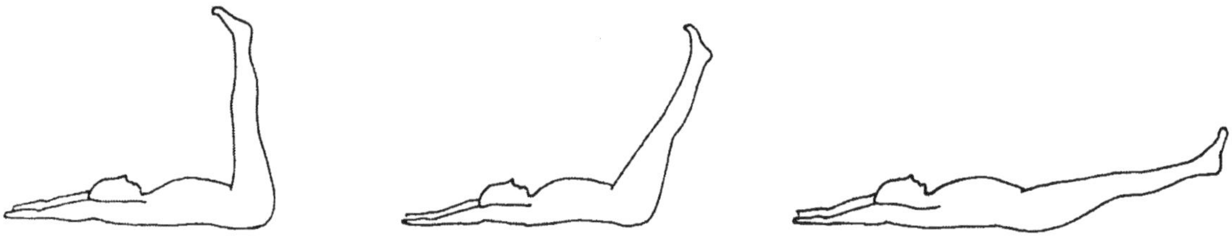

Ūrdhva Prasārita Pādāsana

Jaṭhara Parivartanāsana

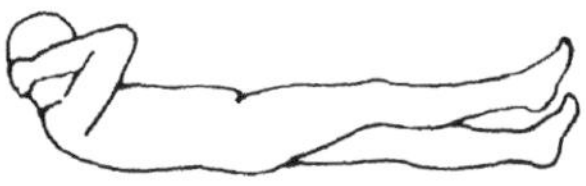

Eka Pāda Ardha Nāvāsana

Ardha Nāvāsana

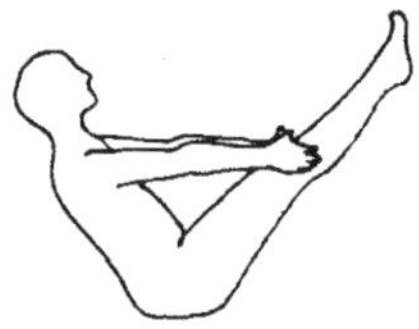

Paripūrṇa Nāvāsana

ŚĪRṢĀSANA CYCLE

1. **Sālamba Śīrṣāsana I** - 5-15 minutes
   sa=with; ālamba=support; śirṣa=head
2. **Parivṛtta Śīrṣāsana** - 1 minute
   parivṛtta=turned around
3. **Parivṛtta Eka Pāda Śīrṣāsana** - 1 minute
   eka=one; pāda=leg, foot
4. **Pārśva Eka Pāda Śīrṣāsana** - 30 seconds
   pārśva=sideways
5. **Eka Pāda Śīrṣāsana** - 30 seconds

6. **Ūrdhva Padmāsana in Śīrṣāsana** - 30 seconds
   ūrdhva=upwards; padma=lotus
7. **Parivṛtta Ūrdhva Padmāsana in Śīrṣāsana** -30 seconds
   parivṛtta=turned around
8. **Piṇḍāsana in Śīrṣāsana** -30 seconds
   piṇḍa=embryo
9. **Vajra Śīrṣāsana** - 30 seconds
   vajra=thunderbolt, weapon of Indra
10. **Parivṛtta Vajra Śīrṣāsana** - 30 seconds

11. **Prasārita Pādottānāsana in Śīrṣāsana** - 1 minute
    prasārita=spread, extended; pāda=leg, foot; uttana=intense stretch
12. **Baddha Koṇāsana in Śīrṣāsana** - 1 minute
    baddha=bound; koṇa=angle
13. **Sālamba Śīrṣāsana II** - 30 seconds
    sa=with; ālamba=support
14. **Sālamba Śīrṣāsana III** - 30 seconds

15. **Mukta Hasta Śīrṣāsana** - 30 seconds
    mukta=free; hasta=hand
16. **Ūrdhva Daṇḍāsana** - 30 seconds
    ūrdhva=upwards; daṇḍa=staff.

ŚĪRṢĀSANA CYCLE

Sālamba Śīrṣāsana I

Parivṛtta Śīrṣāsana

Parivṛtta Eka Pāda Śīrṣāsana

Pārśva Eka Pāda Śīrṣāsana

Eka Pāda Śīrṣāsana

Ūrdhva Padmāsana in Śīrṣāsana

Parivṛtta Ūrdhva Padmāsana in Śīrṣāsana

Piṇḍāsana in Śīrṣāsana

Vajra Śīrṣāsana

Parivṛtta Vajra Śīrṣāsana

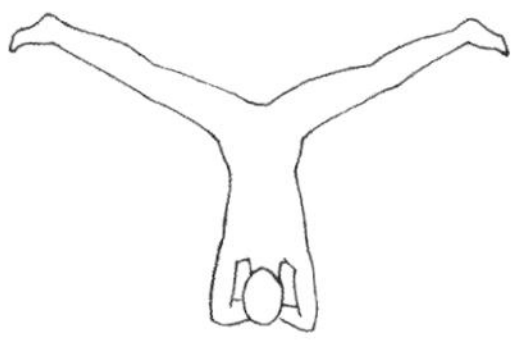

Prasārita Pādottānāsana in Śīrṣāsana

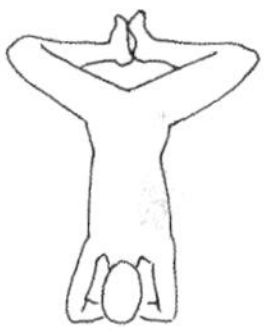

Baddha Koṇāsana in Śīrṣāsana

Sālamba Śīrṣāsana II

Sālamba Śīrṣāsana III

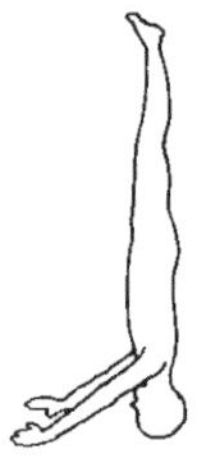

Mukta Hasta Śīrṣāsana

Ūrdhva Daṇḍāsana

SARVĀNGĀSANA CYCLE

1. **Halāsana** - 4 minutes
   hala=plough
2. **Karṇapīdāsana** - 1 minute
   karṇa=ear; pīḍā=pressure
3. **Sālamba Sarvāngāsana I** - 10 minutes
   sa=with; ālamba=support; sarva=whole; anga=body
4. **Sālamba Sarvāngāsana II** - 30 seconds
   sa=with; ālamba=support
5. **Nirālamba Sarvāngāsana I** - 30 seconds
   nir=without; ālamba=support
6. **Nirālamba Sarvāngāsana II**

7. **Pārśva Eka Pāda Sarvāngāsana** - 30 seconds
   pārśva=sideways; eka=one; pāda=leg, foot
8. **Eka Pāda Sarvāngāsana** - 30 seconds

9. **Supta Koṇāsana** - 30 seconds
   supta=lying down; koṇa=angle
10. **Pārśva Halāsana** - 30 seconds
    pārśva=sideways; hala=plough
11. **Pārśva Karṇapīdāsana** - 30 seconds
    karṇa=ear; pīḍā=pressure
12. **Pārśva Sarvāngāsana**

13. **Pārśva Setu Bandha**
    setu=bridge; setu bandha=the construction of a bridge
14. **Ūrdhva Padmāsana in Sarvāngāsana** - 30 seconds
    ūrdhva=upwards; padma=lotus
15. **Pārśva Ūrdhva Padmāsana in Sarvāngāsana** - 1 minute
    pārśva=sideways
16. **Pārśva Pindāsana in Sarvāngāsana** - 1 minute
    piṇḍa=embryo
17. **Pindāsana in Sarvāngāsana** - 30 seconds

SARVĀNGĀSANA CYCLE

Halāsana

Karṇapīdāsana

Sālamba Sarvāngāsana I

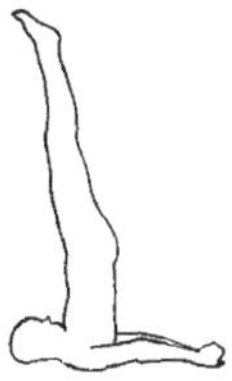

Sālamba Sarvāngāsana II

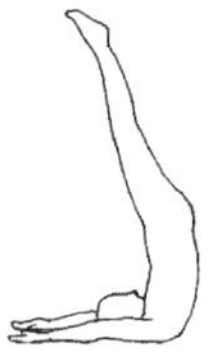

Nirālamba Sarvāngāsana I

Nirālamba Sarvāngāsana II

Pārśva Eka Pāda Sarvāngāsana

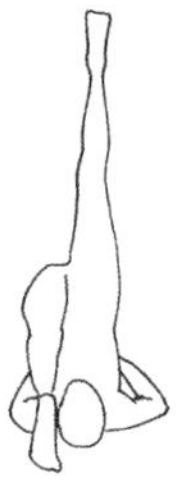

Eka Pāda Sarvāngāsana

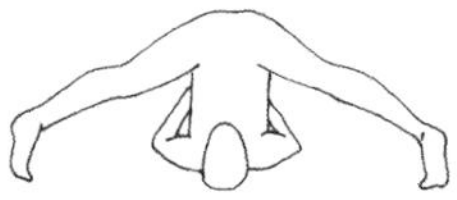

Supta Koṇāsana

Pārśva Halāsana

Pārśva Karṇapīdāsana

Pārśva Sarvāngāsana

Pārśva Setu Bandha

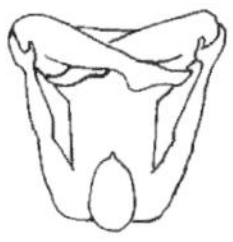

Ūrdhva Padmāsana in Sarvāngāsana

Pārśva Ūrdhva Padmāsana in Sarvāngāsana

Pārśva Piṇḍāsana in Sarvāngāsana

Piṇḍāsana in Sarvāngāsana

SITTING POSES - Full Program

These Āsanas can be done in four different modes:

A. **Performing each pose separately,** and holding it for one minute. To release the knees you can do one minute of Paschimottānāsana between poses.

B. **Vinyasa I** - Connecting two or more poses by flowing from one into the other.

C. **Vinyasa II** - Interlacing all the poses with Sūrya Namaskar.

D. **Taking only the first pose of each series,** and holding it for five minutes each. Here too you can release the knees by doing one minute of Paschimottānāsana in between poses.

Finish the whole series off with 5-10 minutes Paschimottānāsana.

I - PADMĀSANA CYCLE - Short Timing

❖ **Change the crossing of the legs**

1. **Ardha Padmāsana** - 1 minute
   ardha=half; padma=lotus
2. **Padmāsana**
   a. **Padmāsana** - 1 minute
   b. **Parvatāsana** - 1 minute
   parvata=mountain
   c. **Gomukhāsana** - 1 minute
   go=cow; mukha=face
   d. **Namaste II** - 1 minute
3. **Yoga Mudrāsana I**
   mudra=closing,sealing
4. **Supta Padmāsana** - 1 minute
   supta=lying down; padma=lotus
5. **Matsyāsana I**
   matsya=fish
   a. **Matsyāsana I** - 1 minute
   b. **Paryankāsana I**
   paryanka=couch
   c. **Paryankāsana II**
6. **Matsyāsana II**
   a. **Adho Mukha Matsyāsana II** - 1 minute
   adho=downwards; mukha=face
   b. **Ūrdhva Mukha Matsyāsana II** - 1 minute
   ūrdhva=upwards; mukha=face
7. **Parivṛtta Padmāsana** - 1 minute
   parivṛtta=turned around
8. **Tolāsana**
   tola=a pair of scales

PADMĀSANA CYCLE

Ardha Padmāsana

Padmāsana

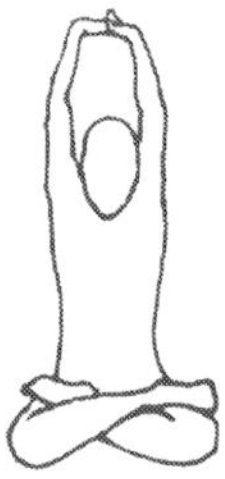
Parvatāsana

Gomukhāsana

Namaste II

Yoga Mudrāsana I

Supta Padmāsana

Matsyāsana I

Paryankāsana I

Paryankāsana II

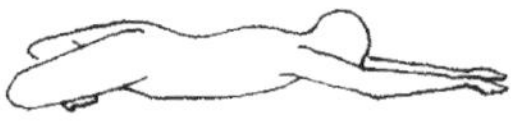
Adho Mukha Matsyāsana II

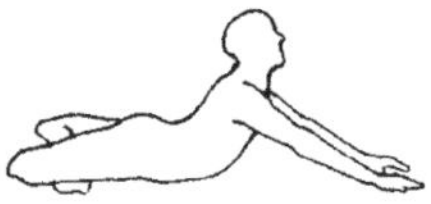
Ūrdhva Mukha Matsyāsana II

Parivṛtta Padmāsana

Tolāsana

9. **Kukkuṭāsana**
   kukkuṭa=cock
10. **Garbha Piṇḍāsana**
   garbha=womb; piṇḍa=embryo
11. **Gorakṣāsana**
   gorakṣa=cowherd, name of a famous Yogi
12. **Baddha Padmāsana**
   baddha=bound; padma=lotus
13. **Yoga Mudrāsana II**
   mudra=closing,sealing

II - VAJRĀSANA CYCLE - Short Timing

1. **Vajrāsana I**
   a. **Vajrāsana I** - 1 minute
      vajra=thunderbolt, weapon of Indra
   b. **Parvatāsana** - 1 minute
      parvata=mountain
   c. **Gomukhāsana** - 1 minute
      go=cow; mukha=face
   d. **Namaste II** - 1 minute

2. **Vajrāsana II**

3. **Supta Vajrāsana**
   supta=lying down
   a. **Dwi Pāda Supta Vajrāsana** - 1 minute
      dwi=two; pāda=leg, foot
   b. **Eka Pāda Supta Vajrāsana** - 1 minute
      eka=one; pāda=leg, foot

Kukkuṭāsana

Garbha Pinḍāsana

Gorakṣāsana

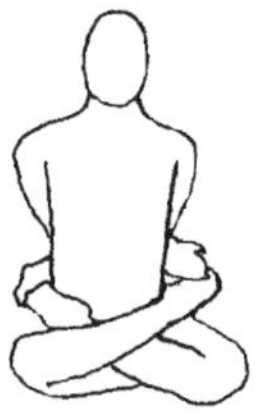

Baddha Padmāsana

Yoga Mudrāsana II

VAJRĀSANA CYCLE

Vajrāsana I

Parvatāsana

Gomukhāsana

Namaste II

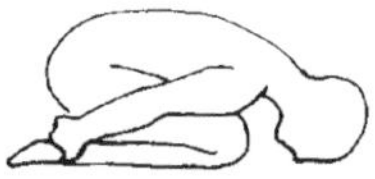

Vajrāsana II

Dwi Pāda Supta Vajrāsana

Eka Pāda Supta Vajrāsana

III - VĪRĀSANA CYCLE - Short Timing

1. **Vīrāsana I**
   vīra=hero
   a. **Vīrāsana I** (knees together) - 1 minute
   b. **Parvatāsana** - 1 minute
      parvata=mountain
   c. **Gomukhāsana** - 1 minute
      go=cow; mukha=face
   d. **Namaste II** - 1 minute
   e. **Upaviṣṭha Vīrāsana I** (knees spread apart) - 1 minute

2. **Gomukhāsana** - full pose

3. **Supta Vīrāsana**
   a. **Eka Pāda Supta Vīrāsana** - 30 seconds
      eka=one; pāda=leg, foot
   b. **Paryankāsana I**
      paryanka=couch
   c. **Paryankāsana II**
   d. **Supta Vīrāsana** - 1 minute

4. **Bhekāsana**
   bheka=frog

IV - BADDHA KOṆĀSANA CYCLE - Short Timing

1. **Baddha Koṇāsana I**
   a. **Baddha Koṇāsana I** - 1 minute
      baddha=bound; koṇa=angle
   b. **Parvatāsana** - 1 minute
      parvata=mountain
   c. **Gomukhāsana** - 1 minute
      go=cow; mukha=face
   d. **Namaste II** - 1 minute

2. **Mūlabhandāsana**
   mūla=root, base, first chakra; bandha=fetter
3. **Kandāsana**
   kanda=root, base of the trunk
4. **Baddha Koṇāsana II** - 5 minutes

5. **Supta Baddha Koṇāsana** - 1 minute

VĪRĀSANA CYCLE

Vīrāsana I

Parvatāsana

Gomukhāsana

Namaste II

Upaviṣṭha Vīrāsana I

Gomukhāsana
Full pose

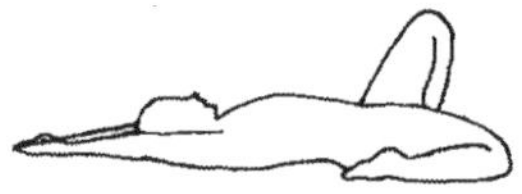
Eka Pāda Supta Vīrāsana

Paryankāsana I

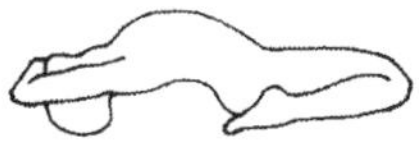
Paryankāsana II

Supta Vīrāsana

Bhekāsana

BADDHA KOṆĀSANA CYCLE

Baddha Koṇāsana I

Parvatāsana

Gomukhāsana

Namaste II

Mūlabhandāsana

Kandāsana

Baddha Koṇāsana II

Supta Baddha Koṇāsana

V - SITTING POSES - Long Timing, five minutes each pose

1. **Padmāsana**
2. **Yoga Mudrāsana I**
3. **Supta Padmāsana**
4. **Matsyāsana I**
5. **Adho Mukha Matsyāsana II**
6. **Vajrāsana I**
7. **Vajrāsana II**
8. **Dwi Pāda Supta Vajrāsana**
9. **Vīrāsana I**
10. **Supta Vīrāsana**
11. **Baddha Koṇāsana II**
12. **Supta Baddha Koṇāsana**

LEG STRETCHES - Long Timing, five minutes each pose

1. **Ūrdhva Mukha Paschimottānāsana II**
   (legs together, holding feet with hands)
2. **Ūrdhva Mukha Prasārita Pādottānāsana II**
   (legs spread, holding feet with hands)
3. **Supta Pādānguṣṭhāsana I**
   (holding right leg with both hands)
4. **Supta Pādānguṣṭhāsana II**
   (with right hand bring right foot to right side)
5. **Supta Pādānguṣṭhāsana III**
   (with left hand bring right foot to left side)
6. **Repeat 3 through 5 with the left leg.**
7. **Samakoṇāsana**

SITTING POSES - LONG TIMING

Padmāsana

Yoga Mudrāsana I

Supta Padmāsana

Matsyāsana I

Adho Mukha Matsyāsana II

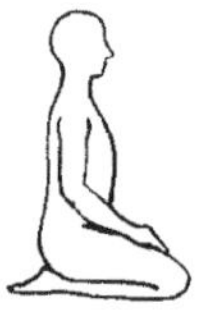

Vajrāsana I

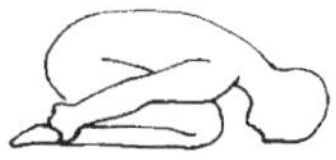

Vajrāsana II

Dwi Pāda Supta Vajrāsana

Vīrāsana I

Supta Vīrāsana

Baddha Koṇāsana II

Supta Baddha Koṇāsana

LEG STRECHES – LONG TIMING

Ūrdhva Mukha
Paschimottānāsana II

Ūrdhva Mukha
Prasārita Padottānāsana II

Supta Pādānguṣṭhāsana I

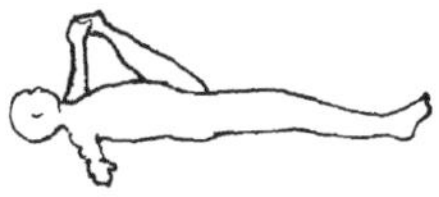

Supta Pādānguṣṭhāsana II

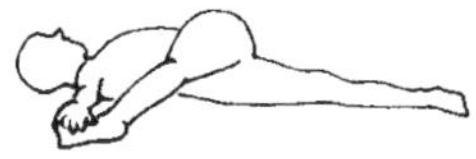

Supta Pādānguṣṭhāsana III

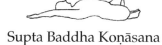

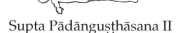

Samakoṇāsana

Reflections

sthāny-upanimantraṇe saṅga-samya-akaraṇaṃ punar-aniṣṭa-prasaṅgāt

'Even then with the invitation of high placed beings, there is no cause for attachment or pride, this because of the undesired and repeated tendency of falling.'

~ ~ ~

'I have just managed to obtain the lamp of yoga which destroys the blindness of the Saṃskāras (imprints)...

Thus confirming his purpose, let him practice Samādhi on it. Giving up all association with them, let him take no pride in being thus solicited by the gods themselves. If he, through such pride, feels himself secure, he will forget that death has already grasped his forelock, and then carelessness - always to be guarded against as it seeks an opening - will enter and rouse the Saṃskāras, with their undesirable consequences. By avoiding that association and that pride, what he has already practiced becomes firm in him, and what he has yet to practice stands right before him.'

The Yoga Sūtras of Patañjali, chapter III, sūtra 51
Commentary by Vyāsa